A
STRAIGHTFORWARD
GUIDE
TO
GETTING THE BEST OUT OF
YOUR RETIREMENT

PATRICK GRANT

Straightforward Guides

ISBN 9781847165190

Printed by 4edge Ltd www.4edge.co.uk

Cover design by Straightforward Graphics

Contents

Chapter 1. When You Retire   7

Chapter 2. Opportunities Available   11

Chapter 3. Taking Holidays   18

Chapter 4. Managing Your Home   25

Chapter 5. Raising Capital from Your Home   38

Chapter 6. Selling Your Home   40

Chapter 7. Extras Because of Age   46

Chapter 8. Future Care Options   55

Chapter 9. Income Tax   65

Chapter 10. Capital Gains Tax   72

Chapter 11. Making a Will   76

Part Two: Finances After Retirement-Pensions

Chapter 12. Pensions and Planning for the Future   81

Chapter 13. How Much Income Do You Need In Retirement?   85

Chapter 14. Sources of Pension   91

Chapter 15. Women and Pensions   98

Chapter 16. The Sate Pension   101

Chapter 17. Job Related Pensions   114

Chapter 18. Group Personal Pensions   123

Chapter 19. New Duties for Employers   125

Chapter 20. Protecting Pensions   129

Chapter 21. Tax and Pensions   135

Chapter 22. Reaching Retirement Age   139

Chapter 23. Continuing to Work   145

Useful addresses
Index
****

Introduction

Most people start to seriously think about their retirement when they reach their late 50's /early 60's. They think about how they can afford their retirement and how they can best spend their time. On average, a third of a person's lifetime is spent in retirement and it is a great opportunity to take up the many things that you have not had the time for.

Of course, it is the case that many people have a very clear idea about what they want to do and how much it is all going to cost. There is suddenly time to do everything that you have wanted, within reason and within financial limits. There are, however, hidden problems that can surface when a person retires. One of these is personal relationships. Retirement can cause stress in people's relationships as you now spend a lot more time together or one partner retires and wants to embark on different projects whilst the other is still working.

People who live alone may worry about losing the day-to-day companionship that goes with the workplace. People also worry about how they may cope as they get older and ill health begins to surface.

This book attempts to cover all areas relating to retirement. The first chapters deal with more personal matters, including management of the home and future care options whilst the latter chapters deal with more financial issues, such as pensions and benefits. All in all, the reader will benefit from this highly readable book which is packed with information.

Patrick Grant

1

When You Retire

Although people generally look forward to retirement, it is true to say that, in the absence of any grand plans, the experience of being at home can take some adjusting to.

Being on your own

There are increasing numbers of people who find themselves alone when they retire. Many people like being single and have planned their lives around this. Although it is true that having a partner can mean that you have someone to be with and to go on holiday with and do many other things with, some people like to do these things either on their own or perhaps with another member of the family.

However, many people on their own also hope that they can find a partner in retirement, someone to share life with. This can be more difficult for women than men. Older women outnumber men, and men may be on the lookout for a younger partner.

The truth is that, in older age, many people will find it difficult to find a partner. The opportunities get less and less. One option is to contact a marriage bureau or to enrol on a dating site online or to go to a dating agency. If you are thinking about contacting a dating agency, particularly for the first time, make sure that you know exactly what you are looking for-a long term relationship or something less committed.

If you live alone, and don't intend to look for a partner, then you might want to develop your ties in the community. A sense of belonging, of community, is very important so as not to get too isolated and so as to ensure that someone will always look out for you.

Your partner

If you are retiring and have a partner, you will need to involve them in your retirement plans. This may sound obvious but by no means all people communicate with each other clearly when it comes to life after retirement and problems can occur. You will have to decide how to cope being with each other all the time, after spending so much time apart when working. If you think that you may need help with the transition to retirement then you should contact Relate who specialise in this area. Many people see Relate as dealing only with marital breakdown but they specialise in marital problems generally, or potential problems. See useful addresses at the back of this book.

Sexual relations

It doesn't follow that, as people get older so their sex life diminishes or the desire goes away. It is a fact that many people enjoy active sexual relations for many years after they retire. This aspect of life is just as important to older people as for younger couples.

Most people are able to enjoy sexual relations throughout their lives. However, when people get older sexual expression can take many forms. The importance of an orgasm, for example, may diminish. The main thing is that two people enjoy sex in their own way. As long as fulfilment is gained then this is all that matters. Growing older can bring some advantages in relation to sex. Once a woman is past the menopause then the fear of getting pregnant disappears. For many women, the fact that their partner takes longer to reach orgasm is a definite bonus. Also, when people enter the phase of retirement there is generally more time to enjoy and explore sexual relations.

It is also true to say that sexual relationships don't just involve women. Partners of the same sex equally enjoy sexual relationships as they get older.

Enhancing your sex life

Although, as discussed, people of all ages enjoy active sex lives, it is true to say that for some older people sex becomes less and less frequent. Some people eventually give up altogether, for a variety of reasons, the main one being the loss of interest in one's partner. This should also be handled in the right way. Life together doesn't have to be dominated by sex. If both parties feel comfortable without sex then so be it. The important thing is to maintain good relationships.

There are, however, a few tips which may help stimulate your sex life. A complete change of scene can be exciting. Making love in a hotel room, making love at different times of the day, watching a film can all be aides to a better sex life. You might also want to consider sexual therapy, such as Sensate Focusing, which was pioneered in America by Masters and Johnson. The treatment consists of three phases. During the first phase the couple will be tactile, told to stroke each others bodies, apart from the genitals, telling each other what they like or dislike. At this stage, the therapist will recommend that there is no sexual intercourse. The second stage allows genital stimulation and the third stage full intercourse. If you feel that you would like to explore sexual therapy more, either through the NHS or privately you should contact the British Association for Sexual and Relationship Therapy, (BASRT) www.basrt.org.uk address at the end of the book. Age UK also has a publication called Intimate Relations: Living and Loving in Later Life. See addresses at the end of the book.

****

2

Opportunities Available

When you retire you will find that you have a lot more time on your hands, and it is yours to do as you choose. There are many opportunities. People retiring today live longer and will spend, or could spend, almost as much time retired as working. The fact that you will have so much time in retirement means that it is very important that you make the best use of it.

Learning opportunities

When you are retired you can set your goals however you want and one very useful way to use your time is to embark on a course of learning. You can study for your own personal satisfaction, studying, for example, politics and current affairs, philosophy or information technology. You may want to study informally or to obtain specific qualifications, such as GCSE. Another aspect of attending classes, either in the day or in the evening is that you will meet like-minded people. Because of age discrimination legislation contained within the 2010 Equalities Act, colleges and universities cannot refuse people entry to courses on the grounds of age, so the opportunities are limitless.

Informal ways of learning
Libraries

Libraries are a good place to find out what courses are happening in your area. Many libraries have also set up open learning centres where access to computers and the Internet is free, or at a very low cost.

Museums and galleries

As well as visiting museums and galleries you will also find that you can attend courses, lectures and various events organised by their education department for interested adults.

Radio and Television

Many radio and TV programmes are educational and certain programmes are dedicated to education, such as the Discovery channel. The Open University also has some very interesting programmes, based around their curriculum.

The Internet

This is, without doubt, a very convenient way to learn with almost every subject under the sun being available. If you are experienced and have used the Internet, and almost every one has nowadays, then you will have access to a rich variety of subjects.

If you are new to computers and would like to enrol on a course to learn more, you should try to find the one that best suits your needs. You might want to contact Digital Unite which is an organisation that offers computer training to the over 50's. It has a national network of older trainers. www.digitalunite.com 0800 228 9272.

In addition, many Age UK groups and organisations offer Internet and computer taster sessions in various community locations. You can contact Age UK's information line 0800 169 65 65 or see the website www.ageuk.org.uk.

Attending classes locally

One of the most beneficial ways of learning is to attend a class near your home. There are a variety of classes, run by Local authority adult education services, Worker Educational Associations and others. The University of the Third Age is a useful organisation where activities are all arranged by members themselves, often being carried out in people's homes. The term 'university' is misleading, as no qualifications and exams are involved. There are more than 500 groups in the UK (see useful addresses at the back of the book). Learn Direct can also provide useful information about all areas of education and learning. You should phone 0800 101901 for more information or go onto their website www.learndirect.com.

Learning away from home

If you are not interested in committing yourself to a longer course then there is also the option of short residential courses, providing you can afford the fees. There are a variety of courses, from summer schools in colleges or universities and also field study centres. You can find information in local papers, travel agencies or in the Time to Learn Directory for which you have to pay. This is published twice a year by City and Guilds (see useful addresses at rear of book) or available online.

The National Institute of Adult Continuing Education (NIACE) www.niace.org.uk also offers useful information (see useful addresses).

Distance learning

'Distance learning' refers to learning by post, radio, email, television or the Internet. Although not everyone's cup of tea, it can be a useful form of learning. The main advantage is the flexibility as regards the contents and duration of the course. The Open University www.openac.uk is perhaps the most famous of the distance learning organisations, where you can study for a degree (or not). The University offers a vast range of courses. See useful addresses for more information. The Open College of Arts www.oca-uk.com provides home study courses in a wide range of arts subjects, including music, photography and creative writing. The National Extension College (NEC) www.nec.ac.uk offers a wide variety of courses-from maths to bird watching including courses specifically geared to the needs of people who left school without qualifications and have not studied for some time, if at all.

The Association of British Correspondence Colleges www.homestudy.org.uk can provide lists of colleges and courses. For all of the above see useful addresses at the end of the book. For general information on distance learning courses, or to check the credentials of a course provider, contact the Open and Distance Learning Quality Council (ODLQC) www.odlqc.org.uk See useful addresses. In Scotland you should visit www.skillsdevelopmentscotland.co.uk

Taking a degree

Many universities and colleges will accept mature students on the basis of their experience rather than any formal paper qualifications. Many universities and colleges have foundation courses which can be taken prior to enrolling for a degree course. You will need to pay fees for taking a degree although if you are on a low income then you may qualify for assistance. Students of any age may apply for a student loan to help with tuition fees. However, you can only get a loan to help with living costs if you are under 60 years of age (England and Wales).

The government website www.direct.gov.uk has helpful information about financing adult learning. General information about funding and concessions is available from Learndirect on 0800 101901.

For most people enrolling at the Open University, there is no need for any prior qualifications. However, OU students do not qualify for grants. An OU degree will usually take a little longer than a full time university based degree because of the nature of the learning process. It can take between 4-6 years to complete although this is dependent on the individual student.

For more information go to the OU website www.open.ac.uk or phone 01908 274066.

Getting involved in the community

Whilst people are at work, time for getting involved in community activities is limited. However, when you reach retirement age, there is adequate opportunity to get involved. Becoming involved in the local community can be very rewarding indeed and can be life changing in terms of who you meet and the activities that you get involved in.

Joining a local club or society

The best source of information concerning the type of club and the whereabouts is the local library. Before committing yourself to join any club you should take a look at the programme and attend an initial meeting as a guest. This will help you get an idea of the club/societies activities and to make a decision whether you want to give more of your time. Once involved you will meet many people with similar interests as you and this can be very rewarding.

Clubs for older people

Many of the larger employers will run clubs for ex-employees. These might be the civil service or NHS for example. Local Age UK's will provide information about different clubs and societies. In addition, active older people are always required as volunteers.

Women's clubs

The traditional idea of the women's institute, that of elderly and stuffy people is no longer anywhere near the truth. Today's WI's are very stimulating and can offer a range of activities for members. If you want more information contact the National Federation of Women's Institutes www.nfwi-records.org.uk at the address at the rear of this book.

Working as a volunteer

If you have the energy and the time then working as a volunteer can be very rewarding indeed. It can enable you to put to good use the skills that you have acquired at work, and to keep your hand in. Alternatively, it can give you the opportunity to do something totally different. The opportunities for doing voluntary work are endless. The following gives you some idea of the range of volunteering jobs. You could:

- Act as a guide or steward in a museum or stately home-the National Trust is always in need of volunteers
- Train to be a counsellor for organisations such as Relate, the Salvation Army or Victim Support
- Work with children and young people in a variety of settings
- Work with older people
- Help run a charity shop
- Become an advocate for a Citizens Advice Bureau.
- Become a magistrate or local councillor
- Sit on tribunals
- Participate in governing bodies such as a school governing body

You need to think about what you have to offer and what you really want to do and how much time you want to devote to voluntary work. As stated, it can be a very rewarding experience. You can find voluntary work through a variety of different mediums, such as Age Concern, libraries, The National Association For Voluntary and Community action (NAVCA), www.navca.org.uk volunteer centres, REACH www.reachskills.org.uk (which recruits volunteers with managerial and technical backgrounds) (see useful addresses) and the Retired and Senior Volunteer Programme www.csv-rsvp.org.uk which recruits volunteers over the age of 50. For more information about VSO (Volunteering Overseas) www.vso.org.uk see useful addresses. WORKING FOR A CHARITY www.wfac.org.uk offers training courses for people who want to volunteer in the charitable sector. See useful addresses.

****

3

Taking Holidays

For most people who are working, holidays are confined to a few weeks a year. For those with children, holidays are usually limited to school holidays. However, once you are retired, money permitting, the choices are that much greater. There is more freedom and flexibility to plan holidays around off-peak times and also to stay away longer.

In addition, your priorities may change. Whereas when holidays were limited to a few weeks a year, sun, sand and sea may have been the destination. The possibilities are greater when you are retired.

The various holidays available
Activity holidays

In retirement you may be looking for something more stimulating than lying around on a beach (not that all people do that). Activity holidays have a special appeal and there are a number of possibilities.

Special-interest holidays

These are run by many operators. Details can be found in various media, such as special interest magazines or from Tourist Boards, Tourist Information Centres or from travel agents. These holidays cover a whole range of activities, including, for example, sports holidays, arts and crafts, outdoor pursuits, from canoeing to potholing, history tours, cooking, music and languages. These are just a few. There will almost certainly be something for everyone. Another option may be working holidays and the Conservation

Volunteers www.greentraveller.co.uk is one example of an organisation that runs working holidays.

Town twinning exchanges with European counterpart towns are organised by local groups. If the town that you live in has a European Twin (or any other twin for that matter) you should approach your local council for more details.

Cycling holidays are one of the best ways to explore the countryside. Careful planning is needed here because obviously a lot will depend on your own personal capacity. Look at maps to ensure that you choose a route that isn't littered with steep hills. The National Cycling Charity www.ctc.org.uk can provide information on cycling tours and routes in this country and abroad.

Walking holidays are another good way to see the countryside. The Ramblers Association www.ramblers.org.uk offer walking holidays. All holidays are carefully graded, ranging from the easy to the hard. The Ramblers can also assist if you would like a walking companion. Walking Women (see useful addresses) arranges women's walking holidays in the UK and abroad. Many women decide to go on their own.

Reunion holidays are well worth considering if you have relatives abroad. It might be worth joining a 'friendship club' —membership of Lion World Travel/Friendship Associations, for example, www.friendship-associations.co.uk entitles you to newsletters and discount flights for reunions in Australia, South Africa and New Zealand (see useful addresses).

Specialist tour operators

There are a growing number of tour operators offering specialist holidays for older people. Also, the Internet has a significant number of companies which offer specialist holidays. The Internet can also be cheaper. Also, local Age UK organisations and other groups run their own holidays, usually for more active older people.

Holidays for the single person

As we all know, on many fronts holidays can pose a number of problems for the single traveller. The main one, of course, is the absence of a companion. However, many holiday prices are built around two people travelling. The single person supplement can add a significant amount to a holiday.

One way around this is to go on an activity holiday, as detailed above. However, this isn't the ideal solution if you enjoy travelling around at your own pace on an itinerary designed by you. One company, Solitair Holidays www.solitairhols.co.uk offers singles holidays for weekends and longer breaks. There are also other companies that offer singles holidays and these can be best sourced on the internet.

Long-stay holidays

Long stay holidays are best taken when everyone else is working. They are cheaper and less overrun in these periods. April, May, September and October are the best months. Some special long-stay holidays are available during the winter months often at very cheap rates.

A long stay package may be the best option if it is the first time that you are embarking on such a holiday. It can also be a good bet if you are considering relocating abroad and want a taste of the country that you intend moving to. Some package holidays offer a substantial package of daytime activities and other excursions and also evening entertainment. You could take a car and rent a cottage or farmhouse in a village or right out in the country. Many holiday companies offer such packages to suit your needs.

Arranging your own holiday

If you are independent and prefer to stay that way then arranging your own holiday is obviously the best way to ensure that you can suit yourself.

Finding your own accommodation can be done as you go but it is better if you can plan in advance and book in advance. Again, arranging your own holiday can give you an insight into a place that you are thinking of moving to.

Home swapping

If you like the idea of a long stay holiday but can't really afford it, then home swapping may be a solution. You live in someone else's home for an agreed period of time, while they live in yours. When you arrange a swap, it is necessary to make certain arrangements, such as:

- Sort out who pays gas, electricity and phone bills, and also practicalities such as food in the freezer.
- Check the position with your insurance company regarding house contents whilst the visitors are living in the house.
- Leave instructions for domestic appliances and also other information about local buses, shops and facilities.
- Leave instructions concerning contacting contractors such as electricians, plumbers etc.
- Arrange for a neighbour to drop in and make sure all is well.

Voluntary work abroad

Another cheap way to have a long-stay holiday is to work abroad as a volunteer. Voluntary Services Overseas (VSO) takes volunteers up to the age of 75 years old. The usual spell abroad is two years. See useful addresses for more information.

Camping and caravanning

Camping and caravanning is very popular and offers greater flexibility when travelling around. This is just the sort of freedom that many people want. It also can work out cheaper in the long run once you have invested in all the equipment. If you have never been camping or caravanning, it is better to try a short package holiday first. Many people, in a fit of enthusiasm, have invested in expensive equipment only to never use it again. The same goes with camper vans. Always hire to begin with to see whether it is for you or not. If you enjoy the experience of camping or caravanning then you can always join the Camping and Caravan Club www.campingandcaravaningclub.co.uk

Medical care abroad

It is important, if you intend to travel abroad, that you are well aware of the healthcare situation in respective countries. You will need to check with your own doctor about the vaccinations that may be needed in different countries. You are covered by the NHS for medical treatment only while you are in the UK. If you fall ill whilst you are on holiday abroad, you may have to pay all or part of the cost of treatment. Obviously, medical insurance is a must.

There are special arrangements with many European countries by which you may be entitled to free or reduced cost state treatment. To ensure that you receive this, you must get a European Health Insurance Card (EHIC) before you go away. The application form is available from main post offices or you can apply direct (see useful addresses).

Insurance

Holiday insurance should be taken out at the time that the holiday is booked because most companies give some cover in the event of cancellation. It may be harder to get insurance as you get older, as some companies impose terms or restrict insurance for those over 70. You need to shop around a range of insurers to get the best deal. You should make sure that you get all the cover that you need. Information about travel and holiday insurance is available on the Association of British Insurers (ABI) website www.abi.org.uk. Advice on taking a vehicle abroad is available from the AA or RAC.

Home security while you are away

In the ideal world you will not want to give the impression that your house is unoccupied. This is an invitation to burglars. There are certain clues that can indicate an absent owner such as:

- Uncut grass
- Junk mail and free newspapers stuck in a letterbox

There is no real substitute for getting someone to keep an eye on your house for you. You can also use a 'home-sitting' service to look after your home whilst you are away. Always tell the insurance company that covers your property if you are going to be away for more than a few weeks. It may insist on extra security precautions if cover is to be maintained.

Can you afford a holiday?

There may be the possibility that you cannot afford a holiday. However, there may be some help available. Your local Age UK, local authority or Citizens Advice Bureau might know about charities in your area that can help.

Holidays for people with disabilities

There are a number of organisations that offer help to disabled people who are planning a holiday:

- Tourism for All www.tourismforall.co.uk is a charity that gives free information and advice on holidays for people with disabilities (see useful addresses)
- Local Age UK's sometimes organise holidays specifically for people who are frail or with disabilities.
- Local authority social services departments sometimes have their own accommodation for older and disabled people.

- RADAR (Royal Association for Disability and Rehabilitation) publishes a holiday guide Holidays in Britain and Ireland (see useful addresses)
- Charities such as Arthritis Care and the Multiple Sclerosis Society, for example, often provide information on holidays, and some have their own holiday homes or organise holidays for special groups.

Holidays for carers

If you are a carer and want a holiday break, it may be possible for a bed to be found in a hospital or local authority care home for the person that you care for. Ask your GP or local social services department. If you need a break yourself you can ask for a carers assessment. Vouchers may be available from the local authority to assist with the cost of care while you have your break. For more information contact Carers UK (see useful addresses).

****

4

Managing Your Home

For many people, when reaching retirement age, an examination of the home that you live in is necessary. You may decide that the home that you live in will not be suitable in the future and you may want to change, probably to something smaller or in an area where you would rather be. It could even be abroad. There is also the option of moving to a care home, or housing for older people. All these options will be explored here. In addition, housing options for those with limited capital will be explored.

In many cases, those who retire and are considering selling their home will have lived in the property for many years, often raising children there. Over the years, many contacts and friendships will have formed in the community. Therefore, a number of questions need to be asked when considering selling up and moving, or giving up a rented home and moving:

- Do you still have an affinity to the area and is it likely to change in the future?
- Are you still near relatives and friends or have these patterns of friendship changed over the years and have your relatives moved on?
- Is your home expensive to run and maintain? How will this affect your finances in the future now that you are retired?

By releasing capital through the sale of your home and downsizing/moving area will this help your finances in the future? The sale of a larger home and the purchase of a smaller property or renting of a more age specific property can release capital which can be utilised as part of your pension plan or for liquid capital to give you a better quality of life in your retirement.

If you do decide to make a move then there are also a few important points to consider:

- Will the property be easy to convert as your needs change with age?
- Is the area that you are moving to convenient in terms of amenities, doctors, hospitals etc?
- Is the area quiet in the daytime or is it noisy?
- Is the property secure?

It may well be worth doing an analysis of the good and bad points of your current home before making any decision. Of course, it may well be that, notwithstanding the good points of your current home, it is simply too large to continue to occupy, too expensive and a move is essential.

When making your decision, it is well worth looking at Housing Options for Older People (HOOP). www.housingcare.org which is a self-assessment form for people wondering whether to move. The form is available from the Elderly Accommodation Council (see useful addresses)

Moving to retirement housing
Retirement housing falls into several categories depending on need. It is usually available for those over 60, although there are a number of schemes which are designed for the over 55's. These schemes usually comprise of a number of flats, some with a resident warden, most with an alarm system connected to a central base which can summon help in the event of an emergency. There are many different types of scheme. You basically get what you pay for and those with a number of services will have a corresponding service charge to match.

Many schemes will have a communal laundry and also, in some cases, a kitchen and dining room where meals can be purchased. A guest room is also usually available.

You may decide that sheltered housing (as it is usually referred to) is the ideal choice for you. The presence of a scheme manager might be reassuring and the company of others in a communal area may suit you. However, before deciding on this option, you need to weigh up the advantages and disadvantages of more sheltered housing. There will be the feeling of being 'herded' together and the loss of independence. If you feel like this you should also see whether you can receive the range of services offered in sheltered housing in your own home.

Renting retirement housing

Most retirement homes for rent are provided by local authorities and housing associations, although not all. There are also a number of schemes offered by the larger private providers although they have to manage to high standards set by local authorities. The Elderly Accommodation Counsel can offer advice (see useful addresses).

Purchasing a retirement home

Retirement housing for sale is usually constructed by private developers although an increasing number of housing associations are also providing this type of accommodation now. Once all the properties in a scheme have been sold then the management of the scheme will be handed over to a private management company or housing association. The management organisation will be responsible for the overall management and service provision. Most retirement homes are sold on a leasehold basis with an annual ground rent (typically £250 per annum) and with a service charge that will depend on what services you are being provided. These can range from skeletal to intensive depending on your requirements.

When purchasing a retirement home it is always wise to buy off a developer who is registered with the National House Building Council (NHBC). The NHBC has a code of practice applying to all retirement homes built after 1ˢᵗ April 1990. If you are seriously considering buying into, or renting retirement housing there are a number of important points to consider:

- As with all housing, is the property in a convenient location and will it cater for your needs when you get older?
- What are the facilities within the scheme?
- Will the new property take your existing furniture or will you have to sell this and buy new?
- Most important, are the managing agents experienced in managing retirement housing?
- Who runs the management association, will leaseholders have a say in running it?
- How much is the service charge and what does it cover?
- What are the other expenses involved?
- If there is a separate sinking fund for future major repairs how do residents contribute to it?
- What are the arrangements for resale?
- Does the lease cover what will happen if your health deteriorates whilst you are in the property?
- Who owns the freehold of the property?

The above questions should be answered by the information provided in the Purchasers Information Pack which must be provided. The NHBC Code of Practice sets out what information should be in the pack.

Although many basic rights of leaseholders have been developed over the years and are enshrined in law, the lease is still paramount in terms of what services you will receive, how they are provided and what they will cost.

Invaluable advice for those living in, or intending to move into, retirement housing is provided by AIMS (Advice, Information and Mediation Service for Retirement Housing) www.firststopcareadvice.org.uk See useful addresses. AIMS provides useful written information, prepared in conjunction with LEASE (the Leasehold Advisory Service) called Leasehold Retirement Housing, Your Rights and Remedies.

Options for people with limited resources

Most retirement housing is sold, as with other housing, at full market value. It follows that when you sell you get the current market value. When you sell your own property and look for retirement housing, you might find yourself in a position of not being able to buy elsewhere. This has particularly been the case in the last few years of spiralling house prices and the general distortions of the British housing scene. If you are in the position of not being able to buy elsewhere after selling your home, there are a few options to consider.

Shared ownership housing

Some housing associations and, increasingly due to over-development, private developers, run schemes where you can part buy and part-rent. There are all sorts of names used to describe this model, such as homebuy, but essentially it is what it always has been, shared ownership. In this case, you buy a percentage of the value of the property, say 25%, and then you rent the other 75%. On top of this there will be a service charge (with flats and some houses). It is not the cheapest way to obtain housing but it ensures that you get your foot on the property ladder. You should make enquiries of your local housing association which will point you in the right direction.

Lifetime lease

Some companies offer a lifetime lease, or occupancy, which means that you buy the right to live in your home for the rest of your life. The properties are sold below the market price but you will probably get very little back if you need to move again. They are also known as life interest plans.

To find out if there are any schemes in your area you should contact your local council or the Elderly Accommodation Council (address at back of this book).

Moving to rented accommodation

If you wish to move home but cannot afford to buy elsewhere, then renting privately is another option. Rented accommodation is provided in the main by local authorities, housing associations and the private sector. It is easier to rent privately than through the public sector as there is quite often a long waiting list for property and your capital may rule you out. However, tenancies in the private sector are usually insecure in that they are let out on assured shorthold tenancies which usually have a fixed duration of six months. If you wish to rent privately you should always try to go for a minimum term of twelve months. Property investors who are holding onto property for a longer term will usually be willing to do this as they are always on the lookout for a good tenant who will pay their rent. Beware of lettings agents who will let the property for six months and then charge you for another six month let. This is an old scam and you should always ask about renewal charges.

Options for existing public sector tenants

If you are already a local authority or housing association tenant, and wish to relocate to another area, you may be able to exchange your home with another council or association tenant. This will be dependant on whether the exchange is suitable, taking into account the size of the respective properties or whether any possession orders or rent arrears exist. The council or association cannot unreasonably refuse the exchange. You will find details of exchange schemes at your local council or by making enquiries to your local housing association. The Internet also has details of several national exchange schemes.

Right to buy

If you have been a council tenant for five years or more you will usually have the right to purchase your property at a discount. The discounts are now more generous, at the time of writing in 2013. You won't usually be entitled to buy your home if you are a housing association tenant, although there are some exceptions such as stock transfers from local authorities to associations where the right to buy is preserved. In addition, the current government has promised to extend right to buy to housing association tenants. You won't, however, be able to exercise the right to buy in housing that is exclusively reserved for elderly people.

Moving to specialist housing

People who are finding it difficult to manage on their own may prefer to move to some sort of specialist housing. In addition to retirement or sheltered housing which has been outlined, there are various types of special housing to suit differing needs.

Extra care retirement housing

Some local councils and housing associations provide sheltered housing that provides extra levels of care. This housing is for people who need personal care services, such as help with dressing or bathing. This accommodation is usually provided in flats and there will normally be a shared lounge and dining rooms where meals are available. Housing in this category is usually run jointly with local authorities and people are placed there after a social services assessment. For more information on such schemes you should contact the Elderly Accommodation Council

Almshouses

Almshouses are run by charitable trusts and in turn provide accommodation for older people. Each charity will have its own rules about the types of people that they house. A few almshouses can provide extra care for vulnerable residents. Residents, as the beneficiaries of charity, do not have the same legal rights as other tenants. The individuals rights will be outlined in a 'letter of appointment' provided by the trustees or the clerk to the trustees. For more information on Almshouses, contacts the Almshouses Association, www.almshouses.org address at the back of this book.

Abbeyfield houses

Abbeyfield provides housing for people in need of sheltered accommodation. Usually this will consist of unfurnished bedsits with shared lounges, dining rooms and a shared garden. The weekly charge will include two meals a day, prepared by a resident housekeeper and also facilities for residents to prepare their own breakfasts and also snacks during the day. Typically, an Abbeyfield resident will be over 75 who is supported by a network of local volunteers. Further details can be obtained from the Abbeyfield Society address at the back of the book.

Housing for those with a disability

Many councils and associations have properties which have been specially designed for people with disabilities. This is referred to as mobility or wheelchair housing. In addition, grants are available for converting existing with disabled access. Councils and housing associations also now build what is known as lifetime homes which are designed to be adapted to peoples needs as they get older.

Living with a relative

If you are thinking of moving in with a relative, or a friend, or if you are thinking of having an older relative live with you, you should always weigh up the pros and the cons of such a move. Some of the things to consider are:

- How well will you get on with the person under the same roof?
- Is there enough space?
- Will a downstairs bedroom be needed?
- Is the housing conveniently situated?
- What are the financial arrangements?
- What are the practical arrangements, such as cooking and washing?
- What would be the implications if you or your relative needed extra care?

You should also speak to your local benefits office about the implications for benefits received when you have made the move.

Moving abroad

Many people dream of leaving the UK and moving to a warmer climate when they have retired. However, the financial climate has changed significantly in the last few years and thorough research is necessary before contemplating such a move. Many people have moved away, particularly to places like Spain, and have returned after a few years, either disillusioned or lonely or having lost money on a property that they have purchased.

It is fairly easy to make enquiries about residency requirements in the various countries. The Foreign and Commonwealth office can provide information and contact details for the relevant consulates or embassies in the various countries. However, before even contemplating such a move, there are various questions that you need to address:

- Can you afford to move to another country? You have to be very clear about your financial situation in retirement. House prices abroad may seem cheap compared to the UK. However, the process of buying can be complicated and some countries, such as Spain, can be problematic. In addition, there has been a collapse in the housing market in Spain due to over development. Caution is advised. You will need to have enough surplus income to live as well so careful planning is needed.

- You will need to think about pension rights and health costs abroad.

- What about possessions? You will need specialist advice about furniture and so on, and the costs of moving.

- Can you take pets? You should always ask a vet's advice first. The Pet Travel Scheme (PETS) allows dogs and cats to re-enter the UK from certain countries without quarantine as long as they meet certain conditions. You can get further information from the Department for Environment, Food and Rural Affairs' PETS Helpline www.defra.gov.uk

- Will you want to find work? You will need professional advice about work permits in the respective countries.

Buying a property abroad

There are property magazines covering homes for sale or rent. Also, property developers are represented at retirement exhibitions. However, a word of caution, you will certainly need professional advice before embarking on a property purchase. It might be useful to buy a book on purchasing a property abroad. You will find case studies of people who have bought successfully and others who have had bad experience. For certain you will need to do your homework well. One useful tip is to ensure that a local agent selling property is working within the rules set by FOPDAC, (The Federation of Overseas Property Developers, Agents and Consultants: www.fopdac.com)

There are also UK firms of solicitors who specialise in the purchase of property abroad. Addresses for such solicitors can typically be found on the Internet.

Repairs and Improvements

One of the most important elements of your home is that of its condition. When you retire or are close to retiring, this presents the ideal opportunity to assess the overall condition of your home and to draw up a condition survey (or have one drawn up) so that you can plan expenditure. It is wise to commence the work as soon as possible after retirement, or before if possible, so that you can still carry out works yourself, without resorting to using building firms. This will save money and mean that you have more control. This chapter also points the way to the various agencies that exist which will give you advice on repairs and maintenance and also funding.

Deciding what needs to be carried out

There are specialist advice agencies, called Home Improvement Agencies (sometimes called Care and Repair or Staying Put) that will give specialist advice to older and vulnerable householders and also to people living in private rented accommodation. They are small scale, not-for-profit organisations, usually managed locally by housing associations, councils or charities. They will usually offer practical help with tasks such as arranging a condition survey, getting estimates from builders (trusted builders) applying for grants or loans and also keeping an eye on the progress of work. They may charge a fee towards their assistance, which is usually included in the grant or loans that you may be in receipt of.

To find out whether there is a home improvement agency in your area, you should contact your local Age UK or the local council housing department or Foundations (the National Co-ordinating Body for Home Improvement Agencies) address at the rear of the book.

If there is no Home Improvement Agency in your area you might want to engage a surveyor to carry one out for you. As these are costly, or can be, you should always ask what the cost will be first. The Chartered Surveyor Voluntary Service exists to help people who would other wise be able to get professional advice. You need to be referred to them by a Citizens Advice Bureau first.

Finding a Builder

If there is no Home Improvement Agency in your area, you should take care, great care, when trying to find a good reliable builder. We have all heard stories of rogue builders who carry out shoddy work and charge over the odds. If you intend to employ a builder, particularly for a larger job, then you should always employ a builder backed by a proper guarantee scheme. The Federation of Master Builders (FMB) offers a MasterBond Warranty: its members must meet certain criteria and adhere to the FMB's Code of Practice. The ten-year insurance backed warranty will add 1.5% to the total cost of a job but is money well spent.

Information on this scheme can be obtained from the FMB website at www.fmb.org.uk.

To ensure that you get a good job done, the FMB recommends that you:

- Always ask for references and names of previous clients
- Get estimates from two or three builders
- Ask for the work to be covered by an insurance backed warranty
- Get a written specification and quotation

- Use a contract (the FMB has a plain English contract for small works)
- Agree any staged and final payments before a job
- Avoid dealing in cash

The FMB has played a leading role in the development of the government backed TrustMark scheme, which is a consumer protection initiative for the home repair and improvement sector. A wide range of traders, including plumbers and electricians, are being licensed to become TrustMark registered firms. For more information contact TrustMark address at the rear of this book.

Financial help with repairs and improvements

Sometimes, individuals find themselves in a position where they cannot afford repairs to their homes. There are, however, various forms of assistance at hand. Local authorities have general powers to provide help with repairs and also adaptations to housing. The assistance isn't always cash based, it can also be provided in the form of labour material or advice. The cash element will usually be either grants or loans. Local authorities will have published policies explaining the various forms of assistance. These can vary from time to time, as many of them are dependant on national legislation and government funding. Below are a few of the types of grants available.

Disabled facilities grant

These grants provide facilities and adaptations to help a disabled person to live as independently and in as much comfort as possible. They are means tested, i.e. dependant on income, with the exception of grants for disabled children. In its assessment, the council will take into account only your income and that of your partner or spouse. If you receive the guarantee part of Pension Credit, Income Support or income based Jobseeker's allowance you will not normally have to make any contribution. People receiving Working or Child Tax Credit (with gross taxable income of less than £15,000) have these payments disregarded as income. The grant is usually mandatory provided that your home needs adaptations to enable you to use essential facilities such as kitchen or bathroom. The maximum amount of grant is £30,000. You can get more information about these grants from your local authority housing department.

If you receive Pension credit, Income Support or Income based jobseekers allowance, you may be able to get a Community care Grant or Budgeting Loan from the Social fund to help you with the cost of minor repairs. However, please bear in mind that changes to the benefit system from October 2013, with the introduction of Universal Credit has entailed the social fund administration being transferred to local authorities.

Social services departments provide funding for some minor adaptation works. They may also be able to help with some types of work not covered by the disabled facilities grant.

If you want to raise capital from your home to pay for works, the Home Improvement Trust may be able to help. It is a not-for-profit company that has links with a number of commercial lenders who provide older people with low cost loans raised against the value of their home. You can contact Home Improvement Trust direct at the address at the rear of the book.

The Care and Repair England publication also provides useful information about organising and financing building works. You can get a copy by phoning 0115 950 6500 or by downloading it from the website www.careandrepair-england.org.uk.

Adapting your home

You may need to make certain adaptations to your home if you or a member of your family needs them, such as mobility aids, to make it easier to navigate the house. There are other areas that can be helpful, such as the positioning of the furniture. Occupational Therapists can give detailed advice. They can assess a person's mobility and their ability to move around and can provide appropriate advice. You should contact your local social services department and ask for an assessment of needs. You don't have to have a letter from the doctor but this can speed things up. Social services should provide some equipment free if you or a relative is assessed as needing them. All minor adaptations costing less than £1000 must be provided free of charge.

For full information about special equipment and furniture, contact the Disabled Living Foundation at the address at the rear of the book.

****

5

Raising Capital from your Home

Equity release schemes

The main principle behind equity release schemes, which enable you to release cash from your home, is that you are offered a lump sum or an income now but you, or your estate, have to pay back a larger sum to compensate the investors (the Equity release companies). This amounts to a longer-term loan which is paid back later with rolled up interest. If you wish to raise money but do not wish to move home then these schemes could be for you.

Equity release schemes come in two basic forms: lifetime mortgages and home reversion schemes.

Lifetime mortgages

With a lifetime mortgage you borrow against the value of your home but the capital, and usually the interest are repaid only on your death or when you move out. Lifetime mortgages can be taken out jointly with your spouse or partner, in which case the loan does not have to be repaid until the second death. You can use a lifetime mortgage to raise a single large cash sum. If you want an income you can draw out a series of smaller sums or use a single lump sum to buy an investment, such as an annuity. The former is more tax efficient because the income from an annuity is usually taxable.

Types of lifetime mortgages

With the most common form of lifetime loan-a roll up loan-interest is added each month to the amount that you owe. You are charged interest not just on the amount that you originally borrowed, but to the increasing balance as interest is added. The interest can be fixed for the whole life of the loan or can be variable. When your home is eventually sold, the proceeds are used to repay the outstanding loan and what is left over goes to your estate. Different providers set different age limits but you must be at least 55 or 60 with most schemes to be eligible for a lifetime mortgage. In addition, the value of your home, less any debts secured against it must be in the region of £50,000 and upwards. If you have an existing mortgage you will usually be required to pay this off with the loan. The amounts that you can borrow will vary with your age. The maximum for a roll up loan is usually about half the value.

Reversion schemes

With a reversion scheme you sell part, or all, of your home, but retain the right to live there either rent free or for a token rent. When the home is eventually sold, the reversionary company takes a percentage of the sale proceeds, or the whole amount if you sold 100 per cent of your home. This means that the reversion company, as opposed to the estate gets the benefit of any increase in value of your home. A reversion scheme can be taken out singly or jointly, in which case it continues until the second death.

As with lifetime mortgages, reversion schemes can pay you a single lump sum or a series of smaller lump sums. Alternatively, they may be combined with an annuity or other investment to provide you with a regular income. Investment income is usually taxable but lump sums from the sale of your home are not. The money that you get when you take out the loan will be smaller than the value of the part of your home that you sell. This difference represents the return to the reversionary company. A key factor that the reversionary company uses in deciding what it will offer is how long it expects to have to wait before it gets its money back. To qualify for a reversionary scheme you will usually be between 65-70. Your home must be in reasonable condition and worth a minimum amount, typically £75,000.

Alternatives to equity release

One of the most common reasons for considering equity release is to raise extra income for day-to-day living. If this is your main motive, you might want to consider ensuring that the other avenues for raising income have been explored. For example:

- Are you claiming all the state benefits due to you, such as Pension Credit, Council Tax Benefit and Attendance Allowance
- Have you taken steps to trace any lost pensions that you might be claiming?
- Are you exploiting the potential of your home, for example taking in a lodger?
- Are you making sure that you are not overspending?
- Are you paying too much tax?

You cannot normally use equity release to raise a lump sum of below £10,000. If such a sum is needed you might want to consider taking out an interest only mortgage. Unlike a lifetime mortgage you pay interest each month so the amount borrowed does not grow.

The main thing with equity release schemes is that you should get good advice, usually independent advice so that you are totally aware of what it is that you are signing up for.

....

6

Selling your home

As we all know, the housing market has undergone is distorted and the value of property has once again increased. However, the wisdom of using your home, or factoring in your home, as a source of income when retirement age is reached, is questionable.

Property prices are just one of the problems if your intention is to sell up to release capital for your retirement. The other main one is that if you are aiming to downsize to a smaller home then the price of this property may not necessarily be that much cheaper than the family home that you are selling. This does depend of course on the nature, size and value of that property. In addition, there are also the other problems associated with relocating, such as getting used to a new area, neighbours and so on.

You should bear in mind as well that there are significant costs associated with selling, moving and buying. This will eat into any equity that you release from your property and should be taken into account. The good news is that stamp duty payable has decreased for most people. Instead of the 'slab' system, i.e. a one off payment you now pay tax on the amount between property bands. For example on a property worth £250,000, given that the first £125,000 is free of tax, you would pay 2% of the remaining £125,000. The system works out cheaper for those who pay more.

The table overleaf will give you an idea of the costs involved.

	COST	EXAMPLE 1. SELLING A HOME FOR £250,000 AND BUYING FOR £150,000	EXAMPLE 2. SELLING A HOME FOR £600,000 AND BUYING FOR £250,000
AS A SELLER			
ESTATE AGENTS FEE	1.5%-2% OF SELLING PRICE	£4375	£10,500
AS A BUYER			
STAMP DUTY LAND TAX	BETWEEN 1-15% OF PROPERTY VALUE	£0	£2500
SURVEYORS FEE	APPROX £500	£500	£500
SEARCH FEES AND LAND REGISTRY FEES	APPROX £500	£500	£500
AS BOTH			
LEGAL COSTS	APPROX £1500	£1500	£1500
REMOVAL COSTS	£600	£600	£600
TOTAL		**£7475**	**£16,100**

Case study

John and Doreen

John and Doreen are selling a £350,000 family home and buying a flat for £200,000. The costs for downsizing are:

- Estate agents fees 1.5% £5250 Stamp duty land tax 1% of £75,000 = £750

- Survey £500
- Search fees, Land Registry etc £500
- Legal costs on both sales and purchase £1500
- Removal costs £600

Total £9,100. The cash realised from downsizing is £350,000-£200,000-£9,100 = £139,900.

The main advantage of downsizing is that you realise the full value of the home that you are selling (apart from costs). Also, if you are selling your own home the proceeds are tax-free.

··················

7

Extras because of age

Free bus travel in England for older and disabled people
Eligible older and disabled people are entitled to free off-peak travel on local buses anywhere in England. Off peak is between 9.30am to 11pm Monday to Friday and all day weekends and public holidays.

The England bus pass only covers travel in England. It doesn't give you free bus travel in Wales, Scotland or Northern Ireland.

Free bus travel in Wales, Scotland and Northern Ireland
There are similar schemes in each of the above countries and you need to apply to your respective local authorities.

Who is eligible for an older person's bus pass?
If you live in England, you will be entitled to a bus pass when you reach 'eligible age'. If you were born after 5th April 1950, the age you become eligible is tied to the changes in state pension age for women. This affects both men and women.

Women born after 5th April 1950
If you are a woman born after 5th April 1950, you will become eligible for an older persons bus pass when you reach pensionable age.

Men born after 5th April 1950
If you are a man born after 5th April 1950, you will come eligible when you reach the pensionable age of a woman born on the same day.

If you were born before 6ᵗʰ April 1950

You are eligible for an older person's bus pass from your 60th birthday if you were born before 6ᵗʰ April 1950.

Disabled persons bus pass

You are eligible for a disabled person's bus pass if you live in England and are 'eligible disabled'. This means you:

- are blind or partially sighted
- are profoundly or severely deaf
- are without speech
- have a disability, or have suffered an injury, which has a substantial and long term effect on your ability to walk
- don't have arms or have long-term loss of the use of both arms
- have a learning disability

You are also eligible disabled if your application for a driving licence would be refused under section 92 of the Road Traffic Act 1988 (physical fitness). However, you won't be eligible if you were refused because of persistent misuse of drugs or alcohol.

How to get your bus pass

In the first instance you should contact your local council (whether you live in England, Scotland, Ireland or Wales, who will tell you who issues passes in your area.

Bus passes in London-the Freedom Pass

If you are eligible disabled or of eligible age and you live in Greater London, you can apply for a Freedom Pass. This gives you free travel on the entire Transport for London network. On most services, you can use the pass at any time. You can also use your Freedom Pass England-wide, but only during off-peak times outside of London. If you wish to use your bus pass on coaches then you should ask the coach company about terms and conditions. For more about bus passes for elderly and disabled go to www.gov.uk/apply-for-elderly-person-bus-pass

Passport

If you were born on or before 2nd September 1929, you no longer have to pay for your passport. You can ask for a refund if you are eligible and have applied for a replacement passport since 19th May 2004.

Health

NHS Prescriptions. Once you reach age 60 you qualify for free NHS prescriptions (Currently £8.20 in 2015/16). If you are eligible you simply sign the declaration on the back of the prescription. Scotland and Northern Ireland have phased out charges for prescriptions. Prescriptions are already free for all in Wales.

NHS sight tests. From age 60 you also qualify for free NHS sight tests but you still have to pay for the glasses and lenses, unless your income is low. You can get free sight tests from age 40 if you are considered at risk of developing glaucoma because a close family member has this condition (or any age if you already have sight problems).

Help with bills

Winter fuel payments. This scheme is in force all over the UK and provides a cash sum to every household with one or more people over 60 in the 'qualifying week' which is the week beginning the third Monday in September. You can use the cash in any way you like. However, it is designed specifically to help you cope with Winter fuel bills. The standard payment is normally between £100-

£300 depending on your situation. If you want more details concerning this payment you should go to www.directgov.co.uk.

Television licence. Anyone aged 75 or over can apply for a free television licence. It doesn't matter if there are younger people in the household but the licence must be in the name of the person aged 75 or over. If you are already a licence holder you can apply for a cheaper licence for the part year that you turn 75. The licence lasts three years at a time and you should re-apply after three years.

Your home

You can get help with heating and fuel efficiency if you are aged 60 or over. You should go to www.gov.uk/browse/benefits/heating.

Repairs and Improvements

One of the most important elements of your home is that of its condition. When you retire or are close to retiring, this presents the ideal opportunity to assess the overall condition of your home and to draw up a condition survey (or have one drawn up) so that you can plan expenditure. It is wise to commence the work as soon as possible after retirement, or before if possible, so that you can still carry out works yourself, without resorting to using building firms. This will save money and mean that you have more control. This chapter also points the way to the various agencies that exist who will give you advice on repairs and maintenance and also funding.

Deciding what needs to be carried out

There are specialist advice agencies, called Home Improvement Agencies (sometimes called Care and Repair or Staying Put) that will give specialist advice to older and vulnerable householders and also to people living in private rented accommodation. They are small scale, no-for-profit organisations, usually managed locally by housing associations, councils or charities. They will usually offer practical help with tasks such as arranging a condition survey, getting estimates from builders (trusted builders) applying for grants or loans and also keeping an eye on the progress of work. They may charge a fee towards their assistance, which is usually included in the grant or loans that you may be in receipt of.

To find out whether there is a home improvement agency in your area, you should contact your local Age uk or the local council housing department or Foundations (the National Co-ordinating Body for Home Improvement Agencies). Address at the rear of the book.

If there is no Home Improvement Agency in your area you might want to engage a surveyor to carry one out for you. As these are costly, or can be, you should always ask what the cost will be first. The Chartered Surveyor Voluntary Service exists to help people who would other wise be able to get professional advice. You need to be referred to them by a Citizens Advice Bureau first.

Finding a Builder

If there is no Home Improvement Agency in your area, you should take care, great care, when trying to find a good reliable builder. We have all heard stories of rogue builders who carry out shoddy work and charge over the odds. If you intend to employ a builder, particularly for a larger job, then you should always employ a builder backed by a proper guarantee scheme. The Federation of Master Builders (FMB) offers a MasterBond Warranty: its members must meet certain criteria and adhere to the FMB's Code of Practice. The ten-year insurance backed warranty will add 1.5% to the total cost of a job but is money well spent.

Information on this scheme can be obtained from the FMB website at www.fmb.org.uk.

To ensure that you get a good job done, the FMB recommends that you:

- Always ask for references and names of previous clients
- Get estimates from two or three builders
- Ask for the work to be covered by an insurance backed warranty
- Get a written specification and quotation
- Use a contract (the FMB has a plain English contract for small works)
- Agree any staged and final payments before a job
- Avoid dealing in cash

The FMB has played a leading role in the development of the government backed TrustMark scheme, which is a consumer protection initiative for the home repair and improvement sector.

A wide range of traders, including plumbers and electricians, are being licensed to become TrustMark registered firms. For more information contact TrustMark. Address at the rear of this book.

Financial help with repairs and improvements
Sometimes, individuals find themselves in a position where they cannot afford repairs to their homes. There are, however, various forms of assistance at hand. Local authorities have general powers to provide help with repairs and also adaptations to housing. The assistance isn't always cash based, it can also be provided in the form of labour material or advice. The cash element will usually be either grants or loans. Local authorities will have published policies explaining the various forms of assistance. These can vary from time to time, as many of them are dependant on national legislation and government funding. Below are a few of the types of grants available.

Disabled facilities grant

These grants provide facilities and adaptations to help a disabled person to live as independently and in as much comfort as possible. They are means tested (i.e.) dependant on income, with the exception of grants for disabled children. In its assessment, the council will take into account only your income and that of your partner or spouse. If you receive the guarantee part of Pension Credit, income Support or income based Jobseeker's allowance you will not normally have to make any contribution. People receiving Working or Child Tax Credit (with gross taxable income of less than £15,000) have these payments disregarded as income. The grant is usually mandatory provided that your home needs adaptations to enable you to use essential facilities such as kitchen or bathroom. The maximum amount of grant is £30,000. You can get more information about these grants from your local authority housing department.

If you receive Pension credit, Income Support or Income based jobseekers allowance, you may be able to get a Community Care Grant or Budgeting Loan from the Social fund to help you with the cost of minor repairs.

Social services departments provide funding for some minor adaptation works. They may also be able to help with some types of work not covered by the disabled facilities grant.

If you want to raise capital from your home to pay for works, the Home Improvement Trust may be able to help. It is a not-for-profit company that has links with a number of commercial lenders who provide older people with low cost loans raised against the value of their home. You can contact Home Improvement Trust direct at the address at the rear of the book.

The Care and Repair England publication also provides useful information about organising and financing building works. You can get a copy by phoning 0115 950 6500 or by downloading it from the website www.careandrepair-england.org.uk.

Adapting your home

You may need to make certain adaptations to your home if you or a member of your family needs them, such as mobility aids, to make it easier to navigate the house. There are other areas that can be helpful, such as the positioning of the furniture. Occupational Therapists can give detailed advice. They can assess a persons mobility and their ability to move around and can provide appropriate advice. You should contact your local social services department and ask for an assessment of needs. You don't have to have a letter from the doctor but this can speed things up. Social services should provide some equipment free if you or a relative is assessed as needing them. All minor adaptations costing less than £1000 must be provided free of charge.

For full information about special equipment and furniture, contact the Disabled Living Foundation at the address at the rear of the book.

....

8

Future Care options

As is well documented over a third of people over 65-74 and over a half over the age of 75 have a long-standing health condition that affects their lives in some way. The ability to carry on living in ones own home really depends a lot on the availability of appropriate care. Quite often this is not readily available, and comes at a cost. Those who are fortunate enough can be cared for by their family.

In 1993, the government introduced policies designed to help more people live independently in their own homes through the expansion of formal support services. This has had the effect of reducing the number of people who need care home support.

However, we are living in an age of an increasing elderly population and there is increase pressure on finances and the ability of government to pay. Whether you are thinking of support in the future for an aging relative or indeed for yourself, there are several main factors that you need to consider and decisions to be made:

- Exactly what form of care might be needed in the future, whether a retirement home or higher level sheltered housing
- Where will the money come from to pay for the care?

We need now to examine the various options available.

Care in the home

Most people would rather stay in their own home and receive the appropriate level of support for their needs. Regardless of your own personal financial situation you have the right to approach social services in your local authority area for a needs assessment. Then a manager from the department will visit you in your home (or relative as case may be) and put together a care plan for you.

The whole approach to care in the home and care in residential homes has been redefined by the Care Act 2014, a summary of which is below.

The Care Act 2014

The *Care Act 2014* came into force on 1st April 2015 along with a range of new supporting regulations and a single set of statutory guidance, which, taken together, describe how the Act should be applied in practice. The aim of the change is to simplify and modernise the system, which had become very complex and also to create a new approach to charging. The *Care Act 2014* will actually come into force in two stages, in April 2015 and April 2016. Some of the key changes being introduced in 2015 are:

- The promotion of individual well-being as an overarching principle within all the activities of a local authority including: assessment, eligibility, prevention, means testing and care and support planning.
- New national eligibility criterion for both the adult requesting services and their carer(s) leading to rights to services and based around the well-being principle. The previous four local eligibility levels have now become one, set at approximately the previous 'substantial' level. Carers now have an absolute right to have their assessed, eligible, support needs met for the first time; they have a slightly different eligibility criterion to the service user, but are subject to the same means test rules.

- •A person-centred, outcomes-focussed, approach to assessing and meeting needs. Local authorities must consider how to meet each person's specific needs rather than simply considering what existing service they will fit into. They must also consider what someone wants/needs to achieve or do and the effect on them of any difficulties they are having.

- The whole system is now administered via personal budgets and based on the principles of the personalisation policy that has been developed over the past few years.

- •A 'right to request' service provision for a fee where someone with eligible needs is found to be a self-funder (must pay the whole cost of a service) in the means test. This right does not exist for care home provision.

- New local authority 'market shaping' duties to ensure adequate, diverse, good quality, local service provision.

- The duty to prevent, reduce and delay the need for services and also related duties to integrate care with the NHS where this benefits a service user.

- A lifetime care cost cap (£72,000 in 2016) above which the State will meet the cost of paying a person's eligible social care needs. The national cap will be reviewed every five years.

- The introduction of care accounts, which will require a local authority to track a person's personal expenditure towards meeting their eligible social care needs, towards the new care cost cap —based on the amount set out in their personal budget. Each account will be adjusted annually in line with the national rise in average earnings. Some local authorities may start to assess for care accounts ahead of the April 2016 start date to avoid capacity issues.

- An increased upper capital limit from £23,250 to £27,000 for non-residential care and support. This includes sheltered accommodation and supported living schemes, which are treated differently to care homes in the means test rules.

- An increased tariff income/lower capital limit from £14,250 to £17,000. You should be allowed to keep capital below this level.

- Independent personal budgets for those people with assessed, eligible, needs but who have capital in excess of the upper threshold and who are meeting the cost of their care and support themselves. This is a choice that will be available to enable payments to be noted in the person's care account.

There are a wide range of support services that can be provided to help you stay in your own home and also to assist your carer if you have one. Services could include: domiciliary (home) carer and personal assistants; meals delivered at home; day center attendance and respite care; live-in care services; rehabilitation services; sheltered accommodation and supported living; shared lives services; other housing options; community support; counseling; direct payment support organisations; information, brokerage and advice services1. Other forms of assistance could include the provision of specialist disability equipment, adaptations to your home, community alarms and other types of assistive technology.

For more detailed and specific information about the changes and new criteria introduced in the Care Act you should go to www.ageuk.org.uk they have ready prepared fact sheets which will help you to see what you are entitled to.

There are certain fundamental rules that local authorities must abide by. Charges should not reduce the income that a person has left below a set level. If a person is 60 or over, this is the Pension Credit

Guarantee credit level plus a buffer which is dependant where you live in the UK, for example 25% in England and 35% in Wales.

The assessment should be based only on your income and generally not that of your partner or anyone else. If you feel that you are paying too much for your care services then you have the right to ask the local authority to review your financial assessment.

How the care is paid for

Either the local authority will pay you direct in cash for your services or, if you so desire, you can ask the local authority to arrange and pay for the care. The Government has also new scheme called Individual Budgets, arising out of the Care Act 2014, which are similar to Direct Payment, so you receive a cash sum, but it covers a wide range of services so it includes, for example, help towards a warden in sheltered housing. The aim of cash payments is to put the individual in more control of the services that they buy. Obviously, this may not be suited to everyone and some people will be more reliant on the local authority to provide and pay for services.

Other benefits available

There are other benefits available such as personal independence payment (replacing Disability Living allowance for those up to age 64) or if you are over 65 Attendance Allowance. These benefits are tax-free and are not means tested. If you are a carer, you will also have the right to a free needs assessment to pay for extra levels of need.

The care plan devised by the local authority might for example recommend that someone be paid for sitting with a relative whilst you have a few hours off, or respite care (where the disabled person moves temporarily into a care home). You will be expected to pay for these services unless your income and savings are low .

Retirement housing

Retirement housing is known by a number of different names that usually reflects the level of care needed, for example sheltered housing, warden assisted housing or warden controlled housing. This is designed for people over 60 (sometimes can be 55). Usually, it is a scheme that comprises a number of flats and maybe a few bungalows with communal areas for residents, such as lounge and gardens and in some cases a kitchen for the provision of communal meals. There is also usually a laundry area and an emergency call system plus a warden if included in the overall scheme cost.

Some schemes are private, people buy a lease, known as leasehold schemes for the elderly. Sheltered housing to rent is normally provided by local authorities and, more usually now, housing associations. To qualify for these schemes you have to prove that you are in need and cannot afford to buy. You may qualify for Housing Benefit.

The main cost associated with retirement housing, whether rented or owned, is the service charge. As an ex-care home manager myself, I have long experience of the difficulties that surround service charges.

The service charge covers the cost of wardens, communal areas, emergency call system and gardening. Many other areas are included. If you are on a low income then you might be eligible for housing benefit for some of the services.

Ordinary sheltered housing does not include care services, this has to be arranged with your local authority. However, as discussed, sheltered housing can be more intensive and the levels of charges will reflect this. For example do you, or a relative envisage needing intensive care of a kind provided by category one sheltered housing or will you need a lesser degree of care?

Moving to a care home

If you move to a care home to receive personal care you may have to pay some or all of the fees yourself, depending on your income. If your main aim is health care, the NHS should pay. This is called NHS continuing care. In some circumstances, you may receive care at home either to avoid admission to hospital or to enable you to leave hospital early. In this case, you are entitled to free care-called intermediate care-which may include a mix of health and social care. The social care element should be free for a maximum of six weeks.

If your primary reason for moving to a care home is for help with personal care such as getting up, going to bed, bathing and so on, in general you are expected to pay for the fees yourself unless your income and savings are low. In that case, the local authority will carry out a financial assessment to determine whether you should pay anything at all. This assessment is in line with the capital limits which can be obtained from your local authority.

Even if your main need is personal care, you may require some nursing care as well and this is provided free, up to set limits depending where you live in the UK and, in England, on the extent of the nursing care that you need. For 2015/16 the limits are:

- England: a standard rate of £112 a week and a higher rate of £154.14 depending on the extent of nursing care that you need
- Wales, Scotland and Northern Ireland will differ.

The Government pays these sums direct to your care provider. If you are paying for your care home fees yourself, you are likely to qualify for Attendance Allowance. If the NHS or local authority is paying for some or all of the fees, you will not be able to get Attendance Allowance as well.

As described above, the Care Act 2014 has affected the way in which home care and care home funding is allocated and you should contact Age UK to find out more.

Assessing your finances

Whether or not you can get state funding depends in part on how much capital you have. Capital includes savings and investments but can also include your house, However, if your partner (married or not), an elderly or disabled relative or a child under 16 still lives there, the value of your home is disregarded. The local authority also has the discretion to ignore your home, if, for example, you carer will carry on living there.

If you are a couple, the local authority is not allowed to base the financial assessment on your joint resources. It must consider only the capital and income that belongs to you. If you are holding assets on behalf of someone else you must prove that they are not your assets or the local authority will treat them as your assets. You can be treated as still owning capital if you are deemed to have deliberately deprived yourself of it. This could be the case if you have given away assets to other family members in advance of applying for a care assessment. Spouses and civil partners are in law liable to support each other and can be asked to contribute towards fees, but the local authority should not do this if it would cause financial hardship. The local authority cannot ask an unmarried partner or other family member to contribute.

Planning ahead for care

If you think that you will need care for a long time, taking out a long-term care product could work out cheaper than the fees. Planning ahead is very difficult and there is no real way to know what your needs will be. There are a few providers of long-term care products and these tend to be expensive. One obvious route is to take out some form of insurance. In the UK, there is just one provider of long-term care insurance. It targets healthy individuals aged 50-70 years. With high premiums (for example around £100 per month for a policy that would pay out a flat rate of £1000 a month it is easy to see why the take up of this insurance is limited.

A handful of providers offer what is known as impaired life annuities that you buy at the point when you need care. You pay a lump sum and in return get an income that pays all or a substantial part of your care costs. The income is tax-free provided that it is paid direct to the provider. The amount that you pay for the annuity will depend on the monthly payments that you need and also the annuity providers assessment of how long that it will have to pay out.

....

9
Income Tax

Tax basics

Each person in the UK is taxed as an individual. Tax is based on income for a tax year. Whilst some types of income is tax free, other income is potentially taxable. Income that is taxable includes earnings from a job you may have, any profits from self employment or business, state and private pensions, some benefits and any other income such as rents receivable, savings interest, dividends from shares etc.

Tax relief can be obtained on certain types of spending which is given in two ways:

- By deducting the expense from your total income, thus reducing the amount of income left to be taxed. This applies to contributions to occupational pension schemes and donations to charity through payroll giving
- Through tax relief at source. You deduct tax relief from the payment you are making and handover the remaining reduced amount. If you are a higher rate taxpayer, you can claim extra relief. This method applies to contributions to personal pensions and chartable donations to gift aid.

Personal allowances

Every individual has a personal allowance. There are annually published individual allowances, which may vary according to individual circumstances. The tables below shows the annual allowances applicable for 2015/16. They also indicate previous years allowances. The allowances are higher for people aged between 65-

74 and higher again for people over 75. However, you will lose this extra age-related allowance if your income exceeds the threshold shown below. The extra allowance is reduced by £1 for every £2 by which your income exceeds the threshold.

Personal Allowances

The Personal Allowance is the amount of income a person can get before they pay tax.

Allowances	2015 to 2016	2014 to 2015	2013 to 2014	2012 to 2013
Personal Allowance for people born after 5 April 1948	£10,600	£10,000	£9,440	£8,105
Income limit for Personal Allowance	£100,000	£100,000	£100,000	£100,000

Personal Allowances for people born before 6 April 1948

People born before 6 April 1948 may be entitled to a bigger Personal Allowance.

From 2015 to 2016, people born after 5 April 1938 get the standard Personal Allowance.

Allowances	2015 to 2016	2014 to 2015	2013 to 2014
Personal Allowance for people born between 6 April 1938 and 5 April 1948	£10,600	£10,500	£10,500
Personal Allowance for people born before 6 April 1938	£10,660	£10,660	£10,660
Income limit for Personal Allowance	£27,700	£27,000	£26,100

This Personal Allowance goes down by £1 for every £2 above the income limit. It won't go below the standard Personal Allowance for that year. There's more guidance about Personal Allowances for people born before 6 April 1948.

Before 2013 to 2014

Before the 2013 to 2014 tax year, the bigger Personal Allowance was based on age instead of date of birth.

Allowances	2012 to 2013
Personal Allowance for people aged 65 to 74	£10,500
Personal Allowance for people aged 75 and over	£10,660
Income limit for Personal Allowance	£25,400

Other allowances

Allowances	2015 to 2016	2014 to 2015	2013 to 2014	2012 to 2013
Married Couple's Allowance - maximum amount	£8,355	£8,165	£7,915	£7,705
Married Couple's Allowance - minimum amount	£3,220	£3,140	£3,040	£2,960
Blind Person's Allowance	£2,290	£2,230	£2,160	£2,100

Tax rates and bands

Tax is paid on the amount of taxable income remaining after allowances have been deducted.

Band	Rate	Income after allowances 2015 to 2016	Income after allowances 2014 to 2015	Income after allowances 2013 to 2014	Income after allowances 2012 to 2013
Starting rate for savings	10% (0% from 2015 to 2016)	Up to £5,000	Up to £2,880	Up to £2,790	Up to £2,710
Basic rate	20%	Up to £31,785	Up to £31,865	Up to £32,010	Up to £34,370
Higher rate	40%	£31,786 to £150,000	£31,866 to £150,000	£32,011 to £150,000	£34,371 to £150,000
Additional rate	45%	Over £150,001	Over £150,001	Over £150,001	N/A
Additional rate	50%	N/A	N/A	N/A	Over £150,001

Dividends

The following rates for tax on dividends apply from 6 April 2010 to the present tax year.

Band	Dividend tax rates	Rate adjusted for dividend tax credit
Basic rate (and non-taxpayers)	10%	0%
Higher rate	32.5%	25%
Additional rate (from 6 April 2013)	37.5%	30.56%
Additional rate (dividends paid before 6 April 2013)	42.5%	36.11%

Allowances for blind people

A blind person's allowance is available if you are registered blind in England or would be unable to carry out any work for which normal eyesight is needed (Scotland and Northern Ireland). In either case, this means that you have been certified as blind or severely sight impaired by a consultant opthalmologist. The allowance is £2,290 in 2015/16.

If your income is too low for you to be able to use all or part of your blind person's allowance, you can request your tax office to transfer the surplus to your spouse or civil partner to reduce their tax burden.

The Married Couple's allowance

This particular allowance is restricted to married couples and civil partners where one or both of the couple were born before 6th April 1935. In 2015/16 the allowance is £8,355, with a minimum amount of £3,220. Married couples allowance works differently to other allowances in that you get a reduction in your tax bill equal to 10% of the allowance or the amount needed to reduce your tax bill to zero (whichever is lower). Married couples allowance is initially given to the husband (if you were married before 5th December 2005 or whoever has the higher income where your marriage or civil partnership took place on or after that date). If the person who has the allowance has income above the age related allowance threshold (£27,700 in 2015/16) the married couple's allowance is reduced by £1 for every £2 of income over the threshold. However, married couples allowance is never reduced below a basic amount (£3,220 in 2015/16). Age related personal allowance is reduced before any married couples allowance. Whoever initially gets the married couples allowance, part or all of the basic amount can be transferred to the other spouse or partner.

Tax-free income

These are the main types of income likely to be relevant in later life that are free from income tax.

Pensions and state benefits

- £10 Christmas bonus for state pensioners and also the one-off £60 Christmas bonus introduced in 2009
- Winter fuel payment
- Pension credit
- Working tax credit
- Housing benefit (note changes to benefits with introduction of Universal credits in October 2013)
- Bereavement payment (lump sum for widows and widowers)
- Council tax benefit (as above changes withy the introduction of universal credit)
- Disability living allowance and attendance allowance (Renamed Personal Independent Payments from 2013)
- Any additional occupational pensions arising as a result of injury at work
- Tax free lump sum from a pension scheme

Income from an employer

- Some fringe benefits, such as employers pensions contributions
- Mileage allowance
- Up to £30,000 redundancy payment
- Up to £3 a week to cover the extra cost of working from home
- Long service award that is not cash and has been given for £20 or more years service

- Lump sum death benefit from life insurance provided through work

Savings and investments

- Interest from National Savings and Investments including premium bonds
- Interest from ISA's
- Interest from savings and bond based investments held in stocks and shares ISA's, CTF's and tax efficient friendly society plans
- That part of the income from a purchased life annuity that represents the return of your capital
- Income from an annuity paid direct to a care provider

Other income

- Up to £4250 from letting room(s) in your home through the rent a room scheme
- Payouts from mortgage payment protection policies and other loan protection policies
- Payout from an income protection policy you have arranged for yourself (but not such insurance provided by your employer)
- Payout to your survivors from a term insurance policy following your death.

··········

10

Capital Gains Tax

Some types of assets do not attract a capital gain. These are listed below. With those assets that do attract capital gains tax, the first step in working out what tax there is to pay, if any, is to take the final value, the proceeds of sale, and deduct the amount you paid, known as the initial value. However, if you give the asset away, or it was given to you, instead you will need to use the market value on the date of the gift. Also, if you began owning the asset before 31st March 1982, you can substitute the market value on that date for the actual initial value. You are allowed to deduct a number of expenses, including the following:

- Costs of buying and selling
- Costs of defending your title to the asset
- Amounts spent on the item to improve its state and enhance its value.

If the final value less initial value and allowable losses comes to less than zero you have made a loss. This must be set against any gains you make on the disposal of other assets during the same tax year. But losses that cannot be set off in this way are then carried forward for use in future tax years.

Reliefs

There is no capital gains tax on a gain or part of a gain that is covered by tax relief. The situations outlined below are common situations faced by people who are retiring:

Retiring from business

If you are self employed or run a company you will need to decide what to do with your business when you retire. There are a number of things that you can do, give the business away sell the business, shut it down.

Giving the business away

If you give the business away to an individual or a trust you and the new owner can jointly claim holdover relief from CGT. This means that any gain that you have made while owning the business is transferred to the new owner by deducting it from the initial value at which they are treated as having acquired the business. When the new owner disposes of the business, the gain is worked out using this adjusted value. Hold over relief is not given automatically and you and the new owner must make a joint claim within five years of the 31st January following the end of the tax year in which the business was transferred.

Selling your business or closing it down

If you sell your business as a going concern or shut it down and sell off the assets within the next three years you may be able to claim entrepreneurs relief. This allows you to ignore 4/9ths of any gain-in effect reducing the tax payable from 18% to 10%. However, the business gains over your whole lifetime (since 6th April 2008) on which you can claim this relief are limited to £1million. Relief is not given automatically. You must claim it within one year of 31st January following the tax year in which the business was sold or disposed of.

Selling your home

In general there is no CGT on selling your main residence. In some situations however, private residence relief might be restricted, for example if you are absent from your home for long periods or use part of your home exclusively for business or have let your home. Some periods away from home do not cause a reduction in private residence relief:

- The first year of ownership in which you might be renovating your home or rebuilding the property
- The last three years of ownership
- Periods of any length when you were working abroad
- Periods when you live in job related accommodation elsewhere
- Any other periods of absence that together add up to no more than three years as long as you lived in the home both before the first absence and after the last.

Losses

Any losses that you make on selling or giving away assets must be deducted from gains made in the same tax year. Once the gains made are reduced to zero, any remaining losses are carried forward to future years. Having deducted all your expenses, reliefs and losses you can, you next subtract your annual tax-free allowance and pay CGT at a single rate of 18% on whatever remains.

Capital Gains Tax free gains

The below are the most common gains and transactions on which you do not have to pay CGT:

- Whatever you leave on death, although Inheritance tax may be payable
- Gifts to your spouse or civil partner, provided that you live together
- Gifts to charity and local sports clubs that are eligible to be treated in the same way as charities
- Your only or main home

- Private cars
- Assets that are deemed to have a life of 50 years or less (wasting assets)
- More durable personal belongings with a personal value of less than £6000.
- Foreign currency for personal spending and British money
- Gambling and lottery wins
- Gains on certain investments, including ISA's or Child Trust Funds, Gilts and many corporate bonds.

****

11

Making a Will

It is often said that the toughest job in sales it to get people to buy fire extinguishers: no one wants to think that they and their family could be caught in a fire which could kill or injure. The same thinking seems to apply to making a will: most people in Britain have not made a will- something which their families could well come to regret.

There are two sorts of people for whom making a will is not just a good idea, but essential: Anyone who is reasonably well off or whose affairs are at all complicated, and anyone who is in a partnership. Unmarried partners (or outside a civil arrangement) cannot inherit from each other unless there is a will: your partner could end up with nothing when you die, unless they can show that they were financially dependent.

There is no such thing in England as a 'common-law marriage.'

The State moves in

When anyone dies without making a will, the law, i.e. the state, takes over. In the extreme case, where you die single and have no other surviving relatives, all your estate could end up with the Crown. And the law is not at all generous to your spouse: if you have no children, your widow or widower is entitled to the first £200,000 of assets and 50% of what remains - the rest ending up with brothers and sisters, if you have any, or with relatives you cannot remember. If there are children, the widow/widower will get £125,000, plus personal assets and income from 50% of the rest;

the children will get 50% when they reach age 18 and the other 50% when the surviving parents dies. If you aim to save inheritance tax, you need to make a will. For 2015-16 the 'nil rate band' is fixed at £325,000 which means that no tax is due below that level, and anything more is taxed at 40%.

How to make a will

So how do you make a will? You can draw up your own using a will-making kit which you can buy from a big stationer or download from the net. That represents the most cost-effective choice and it could work if your affairs are reasonably straightforward. But if you think that your will could be disputed, i.e. subject to legal challenge, then you need to go to a solicitor. That will be a few hundred pounds well spent and you may qualify for legal aid on financial grounds or because of age: you could ask Citizens Advice. You will probably know a solicitor or have employed one in a recent property deal. You will talk to friends or you can contact the Law Society for a list of solicitors near where you live.

Put yourself on paper

Before you go to your solicitor, there are two important things you need to do. Firstly, you need to put yourself on paper - everything you own that is of significant size, including cars, jewellery, property, home contents, bank accounts, shares and life insurance. At the same time, you put down all that you owe, such as mortgage, overdraft and credit card debts. You need to give precise details of the beneficiaries and be very specific about what you are leaving them.

The second thing you need to do is choose an executor, one or two people whose job is to ensure that your wishes are carried out. Your first thought may be someone younger than you (you will need their agreement to act) but there is no guarantee that they will outlive you. If no executor has been designated, the state will appoint a solicitor for you - for a fee. If you go to a solicitor, think about a formula, e.g. a partner appointed by whoever is senior partner of the firm at the time. The executors will need to know where your will is kept, with your solicitor or in your bank.

Time to revisit?

You have made your will, but you should resolve to look at it again, say every five years: people change, as do assets and liabilities. It is a good basic rule to revisit your will when a new child arrives or when you move house. Outside events can change a will: if you were single when you drew up your will, it may become invalid if you get married. But divorce or separation do not make a will invalid, so you might want to make changes. If you just want to make minor alterations, you can add supplementary changes known as codicils. These are added separately and all alterations have to be properly witnessed. If the alterations are significant, you will need to make a new will which will revoke any other wills you have made.

The case for making a will is essentially simple: as Benjamin Franklin said, death and taxes are certain, and making a will means that your family will not have to spend time and energy sorting out a complicated financial and legal set-up. But when you look beyond middle age you have to assess probabilities - you may be out of the country when your signature is needed, you may get ill or you may be injured. We are now talking power of attorney.

Power of attorney

You probably gave your solicitor a power of attorney when you sold your flat; you may have given a power of attorney to your partner when you had to go on an overseas business trip but wanted to buy some shares in the UK. A power of attorney simply gives a person the power to act for somebody else in their financial affairs or in health and personal welfare. (Rules in Scotland are different). The power of attorney you gave your solicitor was probably an ordinary power of attorney, created for a set period of time and for a specific piece of business. That all seems very practical, you may think, but why should you give anyone a power of attorney? The short answer is that if you are away or fall ill, you will need someone to look after your affairs - and that requires a power of attorney. (If this happens and you had not given a power of attorney, your friends and relatives would have to go to court, which would take time and cost money)

Ending the power

When you have given a power of attorney, there are two ways in which it can be ended. You can end it yourself by using a deed of revocation or it will end automatically if you, the donor, lose 'mental capacity.' This is where problems can arise. Suppose you gave your partner an ordinary power of attorney to handle your bank account while you go on your overseas business trip; you are mugged while on your trip and lie unconscious in hospital. Your power of attorney is ended because you are mentally out of action; for the same reason you cannot give a new power of attorney.

Your partner cannot legally access your bank account or have any involvement in your affairs: catch 22? Until last year, the answer to this puzzle was to create an Enduring Power of Attorney. Under an EPA when you were mugged on your overseas trip, your partner and/or solicitor would register with the court and they could then act on your behalf.

New EPAs cannot be created since October 2007 though any existing EPAs can be registered when that becomes necessary.

New lasting powers

EPA's have been replaced by Lasting Powers of Attorney which have separate sections for personal welfare and for property and affairs. Each of these has to be registered separately and the LP A can only be used - similar to an EPA - once it has been registered with the Office of the Public Guardian. If you want to change your mind, you can cancel all the different Powers of Attorney, so long as you are still mentally capable. This may all sound elaborate but it represents the only answer to the situation where you cannot manage your affairs because of accident, illness, age or whatever - but someone needs to do so.

The need for a power of attorney is now that much greater because banks and financial institutions are more aware of their legal responsibilities. Formerly, a friendly bank manager might have been prepared to help your partner sort out what needed to be done while you were out of action. Now, your friendly bank manager is more likely to stick to the legal rules, if only to protect himself and his employer.

You as attorney

One of your colleagues may ask you to be his attorney; if you agree, make sure that a firm of solicitors are also involved. You will have some costs - such as when you register the power of attorney - and there are strict rules, for keeping money and property separate and for keeping accounts of any dealings for the person who gave you the power. When you register, you are obliged to tell your colleague's relatives who are free to object. This is not a job for a layman acting all by himself

···················

12

Pensions and Planning for the Future

Planning for the future

The main principle with all pension provision is that the sooner you start saving money in a pension plan the more that you will have at retirement. The later that you leave it the less you will have or the more expensive that it will be to create a fund adequate enough for your needs.

In order to gauge your retirement needs, you will need to have a clear idea of your lifestyle, or potential lifestyle in retirement. This is not something that you can plan, or want to plan, at a younger age but the main factor is that the more that you have the easier life will be. There are two main factors which currently underpin retirement:

- Improved health and longevity-we are living longer and we have better health so therefore we are more active
- People are better off-improved state and company pensions

Sources of pension and other retirement income

Government statistics indicate that there is a huge gap between the poorest and richest pensioners in the United Kingdom. No surprise there. The difference between the richest fifth of single pensioners and the poorest fifth is about £400 per week. The poorest fifth of pensioners in the UK are reliant mainly on state benefits whilst the wealthier groups have occupational incomes and also personal investment incomes. The tables below indicates the disparity between the richest and poorest socio-economic groups:

TYPE OF PENSIONER HOUSEHOLD

Income per week Single   **Couple**

	Single					Couple			
				603					1451
			327					669	
		256					497		
	216					379			
162				274					

Poorest Next 5th Middle 5th Next 5th Richest 5th Poorest 5th Next 5th Middle 5th Next 5th   Richest 5th

Source: The Pensioners Income Series 2012-2013.

Income sources of poorest and richest pensioners (Single and couple pensioners average)

Poorest	Richest
Occupational Pensions 9%	Occupational pensions 29.5%
Personal Pensions 3%	Personal Pensions 4.5%
Investment income 3%	Investment income 14%
Earnings 5%	Earnings 32%
Other 1%	Other 1%
Benefit Income 79%	Benefit Income 19%

Source: The Pensioners Income Series 2012-2013

The above illustrates that those in the poorest and wealthiest bands have a wide gap in income, in particular in the areas of earnings and investments. The richest have managed to ensure that there is enough money in the pot to cater for retirement. Those in the lower income bands rely heavily on state pensions and other benefits. For more information on the Pensioner Income Series you should go to www.gov.uk/government/collection/pensioners-income-series-statistics-july-2014. There is a whole array of comparisons and general information, most of it quite interesting.

When attempting to forecast for future pension needs, there are a number of factors which need to be taken into account:

- Your income needs in retirement and how much of that income you can expect to derive from state pensions
- How much pension that any savings you have will produce
- How long you have to save for
- Projected inflation

1. Income needs in retirement

This is very much a personal decision and will be influenced by a number of factors, such as ongoing housing costs, care costs, projected lifestyle etc. The main factor is that you have enough to live on comfortably. In retirement you will probably take more holidays and want to enjoy your free time. This costs money so your future planning should take into account all your projected needs and costs. The next chapter includes a few calculations about future needs. When calculating future needs, all sources of income should be taken into account.

2. What period to save over

The obvious fact is that, the longer period that you save over then the more you will build up and hence the more that you will have in retirement. As time goes on savings are compounded and the value of the pot goes up. One thing is for certain and that is if you leave it too late then you will have to put away a large slice of your income to produce a decent pension. If you plan to retire at an early age then you will need to save more to produce the same benefits. We will discuss saving arrangements further on in this book.

3. Inflation

As prices rise, so your money buys you less. This is the main effect of inflation and to maintain the same level of spending power you will need to save more as time goes on. Many forms of retirement plans will include a calculation for inflation. Currently, inflation is at a low level, 0.3% per annum (January 2015). However, history shows that the effects of inflation can be corrosive, having risen above 25% per annum in the past. Hopefully, this is now under control

....

13

How Much Income is needed in Retirement-Planning Ahead

For most people, retirement is a substantial part of life, probably lasting a couple of decades or more. It follows that ensuring your financial security in retirement requires some forward planning. Developing a plan calls for a general review of your current finances and careful consideration of how you can build up your savings to generate the retirement income that you need.

There are five distinct stages to planning your retirement which are summarised below.

Stage 1-this involves checking first that other aspects of your basic finances are in good shape. Planning for retirement generally means locking away your money for a long time. Once invested it is usually impossible to get pension savings back early, even if in an emergency. It is therefore essential that you have other more accessible savings available for emergencies and that you do not have any problem debts that could tip you into a financial crisis. You must then weigh up saving for retirement against other goals that are more pressing, such as making sure that your household would be financially secure if you were unable to work because of illness or the main breadwinner dies.

Stage 2-You need to decide how much income you might need when you retire. There is a table below which might help you in calculating this.

Stage 3- Check how much pension that you have built up so far.

Stage 4-Compare your amount from stage 3 with your target income from stage 2.

Stage 5-Review your progress once a year and/or if your circumstances change.

It is a fact that many people need far less in retirement than when actively working. The expenses that exist when working, such as mortgage payments, children and work related expenses do not exist when retired. The average household between 30-49 spends £473 per week and £416 between 50-64. This drops to £263 per week between 65 to 74 and even lower in later retirement (Expenditure and Food Survey 2012).

However, as might be expected, expenditure on health care increases correspondingly with age. Whilst the state may help with some costs the individual still has to bear a high proportion of expenditure on health related items.

When calculating how much money you will need in retirement, it is useful to use a table in order to list your anticipated expenses as follows:

1. Everyday needs

Item	Annual Total £
Food and other	
Leisure (newspapers etc)	
Pets	
Clothes	
Other household items	
Gardening	
General expenses	

Home expenses

Mortgage/rent	
Service charges/repairs	
Insurance	
Council tax	
Water and other utilities	
Telephone	
TV licence other charges (satellite)	
Other expenses (home help)	

Leisure and general entertainment

Hobbies	
Eating out	
Cinema/theatre	
Holidays	
Other luxuries (smoking/drinking	

Transport

Car expenses	
Car hire	
Petrol etc	
Bus/train fares	

Health

Dental charges	
Optical expenses	
Medical insurance	

Care insurance	
Other health related expenses	

Anniversaries/birthdays etc

Children/grandchildren	
Relatives other than children	
Christmas	
Charitable donations	
Other expenses	

Savings and loans

General savings	
Saving for later retirement	
Other savings	
Loan repayments	

Other

The above should give you an idea of the amounts that you will need per annum to live well. Obviously, you should plan for a monthly income that will meet those needs. You should also take account of income tax on your retirement incomes.

The impact of inflation

When you are planning for many years ahead, it is essential to take account of the effects of inflation. Currently, at the time of writing in 2015, we are in a period of low inflation, 0.3% largely due to low oil prices. As prices rise over the years, the money we will have will buy less and less. For example, in the extreme case, if prices double then a fixed amount of money will buy only half as much. The higher the rate of inflation,. The more you have to save to reach your income target. the table below will give you an idea of the changes in rates of inflation over the last ten years. The ONS supplies figures to 2013.

Yr	J	F	M	A	M	J	Jul	A	S	O	N	D	Ann
2013	2.7	2.8	2.8	2.4	2.7	2.9	2.8	2.7	2.7	2.2	2.1	2	2.56
2012	3.6	3.4	3.5	3	2.8	2.4	2.6	2.5	2.2	2.6	2.6	2.7	2.8
2011	4	4.3	4.1	4.5	4.5	4.2	4.5	4.5	5.2	5	4.8	4.2	4.5
2010	3..4	3	3.4	3.7	3.3	3.2	3.1	3.1	3	3.1	3.2	3.7	3.3
2009	3	3.1	2.9	2.3	2.2	1.8	1.7	1.5	1.1	1.5	1.9	2.8	2.2
2008	2.2	2.5	2.4	3	3.3	3.8	4.4	4.8	5.2	4.5	4.1	3.1	3.6
2007	2.7	2.8	3.1	2.8	2..5	2.4	1.9	1.7	1.7	2	2.1	2.1	2.3
2006	1.9	2.1	1.8	2	2.2	2.5	2.4	2.5	2.4	2.5	3	3	2.3
2005	1.6	1.6	2	1.9	1.9	1.9	2.4	2.3	2.4	2.3	1.9	1.9	2
2004	1.4	1.3	1.1	1.1	1.4	1.7	1.3	1.3	1.1	1.2	1.6	1.6	1.3
2003	1.4	1.6	1.6	1.5	1.3	1	1.4	1.4	1.5	1.4	1.2	1.2	1.4

Office of National Statistics 2015.

Some pension schemes give you automatic protection against inflation, but many don't and it is largely up to you to decide what protection to build into your planning. The first step is to be aware what effect inflation might have. Fortunately, pension statements and projections these days must all be adjusted for inflation so that figures you are given are expressed in today's money. This gives you an idea of the standard of living you might expect and helps you assess the amount that you need to save. Providers of non-pension investments (such as unit trusts and investment trusts (see later chapters) do not have to give you statements and projections adjusted for inflation. If you use these other investments for your retirement then you will have to make your own adjustments. You can do this using the table below.

Value in today's money of £1,000 you receive in the future

Average rate of inflation

Number of years until you receive the money	2.5% a year	5% a year	7.5% a year	10% a year
5	£884	£784	£697	£621
10	£781	£614	£485	£386
15	£690	£481	£338	£239
20	£610	£377	£235	£149
25	£539	£295	£164	£92
30	£477	£231	£114	£57
35	£421	£181	£80	£36
40	£372	£142	£55	£22
45	£329	£111	£39	£14
50	£291	£87	£39	£9

The above should be a good guide. If you require more detailed forecasting you can go to www.ons.gov.uk (Office of National Statistics).

....

14

Sources Of Pension Savings-Options for Retirement

1. The state pension

We will be elaborating on the state pension further in chapter 5. The state pension system is based on contributions, the payments made by an individual today funds today's pension payments and for those who are young the future contributions will foot their pension bill. Therefore, the state pension system is not a savings scheme it is a pay-as-you-go system.

Pensions are a major area of government spending and are becoming more and more so. Protecting pensions against inflationary increases have put pressure on respective governments, along with the introduction of a second tier-pension, the state second pension (S2P). This replaced SERPS. The problems of pension provision are set to increase with the numbers of older people outnumbering those in active work, leading to an imbalance in provision. The biggest dilemma facing the government, and future governments, is the problem of convincing people to save for their pensions, therefore taking some of the burden off the state.

Those most at risk in terms of retirement poverty are the lower earners, who quite often do not build up enough contributions to gain a state pension, those who contribute to a state pension but cannot save enough to contribute to a private scheme and disabled people who cannot work or carers who also cannot work. The above is not an exclusive list. The government has recognised the difficulties faced by these groups and have introduced the state second pension and pension credits.

Pension credits

Pension credits began life in October 2003. The credit is designed to top up the resources of pensioners whose income is low. The pension credit has two components: a guarantee credit and a saving credit. The guarantee credit is available to anyone over a qualifying age (equal to women's state pension age-see further on) whose income is less than a set amount called the minimum guarantee. The guarantee will bring income up to £148.36 for a single person and £226.50 for a couple (including same sex couples) (2014-2015). The minimum guarantee is higher for certain categories of disabled people and carers.

The savings credit

You can only claim savings credit if you or your partner are aged 65 or over. It's intended as a modest "reward" if you've provided yourself with a retirement income over and above the basic retirement pension.

Savings credit is calculated by the Pension Service, which checks whether you're entitled to guarantee credit, then makes a further calculation based on the information that you've provided about your income and capital. You don't have to do any calculations yourself. You may qualify for savings credit if your income is over the "savings threshold". The savings threshold is £120.35 a week for a single person and £192 a week for a couple. If your income is equal to or below these thresholds, you won't get any savings credit. This won't affect any guarantee credit you get.

The maximum savings credit you can get is £16.80 a week if you're single and £20.70 a week if you're married or living with a partner.

The income taken into account for savings credit is the same as for guarantee credit, but various types of income are now ignored. These are Working Tax Credit, contribution-based Employment and Support Allowance, Incapacity Benefit, contribution-based Jobseeker's Allowance, Severe Disablement Allowance, Maternity Allowance and maintenance payments made to you (child maintenance is always ignored).

If your income is still over the savings threshold, the Pension Service works out your entitlement to savings credit.

If you get guarantee credit, your savings credit payment is determined by how much your income exceeds the savings threshold. The payment given is 60% of the difference between the two figures, up to a maximum of £16.80 a week for a single person and £20.70 a week if you're married or living with a partner.

If you don't qualify for guarantee credit, you can still get savings credit at a reduced rate to reflect the fact that your income exceeds the minimum level the law says you need to live on. The same steps as above are taken to work out your entitlement, but the Pension Service will also calculate how much your income is above the appropriate minimum guarantee used for guarantee credit. Your savings credit award will be reduced by 40% of the difference.

Guarantee Credit

The Guarantee Credit element provides a guarantee of a minimum level of weekly income for single people (£148.35) and couples (£226.50). The individual applying must be over the qualifying age (see below for definition), although their spouse can be younger. Before 6 April 2010, the qualifying age for the Guarantee Credit was 60. Since 6 April 2010, the qualifying age for the Guarantee Credit has started rising gradually to age 65 in line with the increase to women's state pension age (and then later to 66, 67 and 68).

The over 80 pension

This is a non-contributory pension for people aged 80 or over with little or no state pension. If you are 80 or over, not getting or getting a reduced state pension because you have not paid enough National Insurance contributions (NI) and are currently living in England, Scotland or Wales and have been doing so for a total of 10 years or more in any continuous period of 20 years before or after your 80th birthday, you could claim the over 80 pension. The maximum amount of the over 80 state pension that you can get is 60% of the full state pension. This is currently £67.80 per week (2014/15).

2. Personal Pension Arrangements

Occupational pensions

We discuss occupational pension schemes in more depth later in this book. Briefly, occupational pension schemes are a very important source of income. They are also one of the best ways to pay into a pension scheme as the employer has to contribute a significant amount to the pot. Over the years the amounts paid into occupational pension schemes has increased significantly. Although there have been a number of incidences of occupational schemes being wound up this is relatively small and they remain a key source of retirement income.

From October 2012, it has been compulsory for employers to provide an occupational pension scheme. For the first time, employers are obliged to:

- enrol most of their workforce into a pension scheme; and
- make employer pension contributions

This will affect all employers in the UK, regardless of the number of individuals that they employ. Anyone who is classed as a 'worker' for National Minimum Wage purposes is included in the new pension regime.

This will be introduced in stages, and each employer will be given a 'staging date' determined by how many employees they have as at April 1st 2012. These will fall into the following periods:

	Staging starting date	Staging end date
120,000 or more	1 Oct 12	1 Feb 14
250-119,999	1 Nov 12	1 April 2015
50-249 employees	1 April 2014	1 April 2015
Less than 50 employees	1 June 2015	1 April 2017
New employers from 1 April 2012	1 May 2017	1 February 2018

The above table provides a summary. Specific staging dates can be found at the Pensions Regulator website:
www.thepensionsregulator.gov.uk/employers/staging-date-timeline.aspx

Stakeholder schemes

Stakeholder pension schemes are designed for those people who do not have an employer, or had an employer who does not have an occupational scheme. They therefore cannot pay into an occupational scheme. If an employer does not offer an occupational scheme (many small employers are exempt) they have to arrange access to a stakeholder scheme. Employees do not have to join an occupational scheme offered by employers, instead they can join a stakeholder scheme. Likewise, self-employed people can also join a stakeholder scheme.

Stakeholder schemes have a contribution limit-this being currently £3,600 per year. Anyone who is not earning can also pay into a scheme, up to the limit above.

You pay money to a pension provider (eg an insurance company, bank or building society) who invests it (eg in shares).

These are a type of personal pension but they have to meet some minimum standards set by the government. These include:

- management charges can't be more than 1.5% of the fund's value for the first 10 years and 1% after that
- you must be able to start and stop payments when you want or switch providers without being charged
- they have to meet certain security standards, eg have independent trustees and auditors.

How much can be invested in a stakeholder pension?
There is no limit to the amount that can be invested in a stakeholder pension scheme. However, tax relief can only be obtained on contributions up to a maximum annual contribution limit (known as an individual's 'annual allowance'). For the tax year 2013/14, this is set at the lower of 100% of an individual's UK earnings or £50,000 per annum (£40,000 from 2014/15) – carry forward of unused allowances may be permitted in some circumstances. It is possible to contribute up to £3,600 per year (including tax relief) into a stakeholder pension scheme even if a person is not earning.

A member of an occupational pension scheme may also contribute to a stakeholder pension scheme. You can start making payments into a stakeholder pension from £20 per month. You can pay weekly or monthly. If you don't want to make regular payments you can pay lump sums any time you want.

Your employer offers a stakeholder pension

The rules for stakeholder pensions changed on 1 October 2012. If you're starting a new job now or returning to one, your employer doesn't have to offer you access to a stakeholder pension scheme. they now have to offer entry through automatic enrolment.

If you're in a stakeholder pension scheme that was arranged by your employer before 1 October 2012, they must continue to take and pay contributions from your wages.

This arrangement is in place until:

- you ask them to stop
- you stop paying contributions at regular intervals
- you leave your job

If you leave your job or change to another personal pension, the money they have paid in stays in your pension pot unless you have it transferred to a different pension provider.

The range of personal pensions

Personal pensions are open to anyone, in much the same way as a stakeholder scheme. These are described more fully later on in this book.

Other ways to save for retirement
Other savings

The government offers certain tax advantages to encourage pension saving. However, the most advantageous savings plan is the Individual Savings Account (ISA) discussed further on in the book. In addition, you might have regular savings accounts, your home or a second home. All of these possibilities must be factored in when arriving at an adequate retirement income.

15

Women and Pensions

It is a general rule that women pensioners tend to have less income than their male counterparts. Therefore, when building a retirement plan, women need to consider what steps they and their partners can take to make their financial future more secure.

Particular issues for women

These days, the rules of any particular pension scheme-whether state or private, do not discriminate between men and women. Whether male or female you pay the same to access the same level of benefits. However, this does not always mean that women end up with the same level of pension as men. This is because of the general working and lifestyle differences between men and women, for example women are more likely to take breaks from work and take part time work so they can look after family. As a result, women are more likely to pay less into a pension fund than men.

Historically, the (idealised) role of women as carers was built into the UK pensions system. Not least the state pension system. It was assumed that women would marry before having children and rely on their husbands to provide for them financially right through to retirement. As a result, women who have already retired typically have much lower incomes than men.

Changes to the state scheme for people reaching state pension age from 6th April 2010 onwards, mean that most women will, in future, retire with similar state pensions as men. However if you are an unmarried women living with a partner you should be aware of the following:

- The state scheme recognises wives, husbands and civil partners but not unmarried partners. This means that if your unmarried partner dies before you, you would not be eligible for the state benefits that provide support for bereaved dependants.

- Occupational schemes and personal pensions typically pay survivor benefits to a bereaved partner, whether married or not. However many schemes-especially in the public sector- have recognised unmarried partners only recently and, as a result, the survivor pension for an unmarried partner may be very low.

- The legal system recognises that wives, husbands and civil partners may have a claim on retirement savings built up by the other party in the event of divorce, but these will be considered along with all the other assets to be split between you and you may end up with a much lower retirement income than you had been expecting.

- The legal system does not give similar rights to unmarried partners who split up. If your unmarried partner was building up pension savings for you both, he or she can walk away with all those savings and you have no legal claim on them.

Changes to the state pension from 2016

From April 2016, the new "flat rate " state pension will typically be £155 a week, but only for those who have paid national insurance contributions (NIC's) for 35 years. Many women will not qualify, having taken career breaks to care for children.

If there are gaps in your entitlement then consider buying some added years of state pension which you can do in the run-up to retirement. The state pension purchase scheme is far more generous than any private pension, provided you live more than a few years in retirement. Be careful, though, that you're not going to be buying years that you'd actually make up through work between now and retirement, otherwise you could end up giving the government money for something you'd have got anyway.

Voluntary NIC's cost £13,90 a week or £722,80 a year, and you can normally fill gaps from the past six years. If you are due to retire after April 2016, check to see how much you will receive at gov.uk/future-pension-centre.

Have you told the government you are a carer?
The good news is that full-time unpaid carers will be entitled to the same pension as those who have worked in a paid full-time job from 2016. However, thousands of women who do not claim child benefit or carers' allowance could miss out.

These benefits signal to the Department for Work and Pensions (DWP) that an individual qualifies for NIC's. Since households earning above £50,000 are no longer eligible to claim full child benefit, many stay-at home mums may go under the radar. Similarly if women are caring for a family member but not claiming carer's allowance their unpaid work will go unrecognised. If you are a carer but don't claim any benefits pro-actively contact the DWP to report your situation. If your household income is over £50,000 you should still register for child benefit in order to receive NIC's.

16

The State Pension

Over 96% of single pensioners and 99% of couples receive the basic state pension. Therefore, it is here to stay. Everyone who has paid the appropriate national insurance contributions will be entitled to a state pension. If you are not working you can either receive pension credits, as discussed, or make voluntary contributions.

The basic state pension is paid at a flat rate, currently for a single person £113.10 per week. For a couple the rate is £226.20, depending on contributions (2014-15). A married couple can qualify for a higher pension based on the husband's NI contributions. If the wife has reached pension age her part of the pension is paid directly to her. If the wife is below pension age, the whole pension is paid directly to the husband.

From April 2016, the amount will change to £144 for a single person, subject to contributions, and will increase to £155-£160 over a period of four years. This is will be known as a 'flat rate' or 'single tier' system and is designed to make the current system more simple and easier to understand. Getting the flat rate however, is very much dependant on contributions.

Basic state pensions are increased each April in line with price inflation. State pensioners also receive a (£10 Christmas bonus-check current entitlement) and are entitled to winter fuel payments. Married women can claim a pension based on their spouse's NI record. Men who have reached 65 are also able to claim a basic state pension based on their wife's contribution record where the wife reaches state pension age on or after 6th April 2010.

Same sex couples, as a result of the Civil Partnerships Act 2004, along with married couples of the same sex, following the passing of the Marriage (Same sex Couples Act) in 2014, have the same rights as heterosexual couples in all aspects of pension provision.

Qualifying for state pension

How many qualifying years do you need to get the full State Pension?

The number of qualifying years you need to get a full state pension depends on when you reach your State Pension age. If you reached State Pension age before 6 April 2010, you normally needed 44 qualifying years if you are a man, or 39 qualifying years if you are woman. If you reach State Pension age on or after 6 April 2010 but before 6 April 2016, you need 30 qualifying years. If you reach State Pension age on or after 6 April 2016, you normally need 35 qualifying years.

Using someone else's contribution record

In some circumstances, you may be able to use your husband's, wife's or civil partner's contribution record to help you qualify for a State Pension.

NI contributions counting towards a basic state pension.

Type of contribution	Paid by	Details for 2014-15
No Contributions but earnings between LEL and PT	Employees	Earning up to £111
Class 1 full rate on earnings between PT	Employees	Earnings between £153 and £805.

and UAP		usually paid at 12% but less if contracted out (see further on)
Class 2	Self-employed	Flat rate of £2.75 per week. Those with earnings for the year of less than £5885 can choose to opt out
Class 3	Out of the labour market and not receiving NI credits	Flat rate of £13.90 per week

Key to abbreviations

LEL = Lower earnings limit: PT = Primary Threshold: UAP = Upper Accruals Point: UEL = Upper earnings limit. LEL, PT and UEL usually increase each year UAP is fixed.

Class 1 contributions

Class 1 contributions are paid if earnings are above the primary threshold. The Threshold, set by government annually, is currently £153 per week (tax year 2014/15). If your earnings are above this set limit then you will be paying contributions at class 1 that build up to a state pension.

The level of contribution is set at 12% of earnings above the primary threshold level up to an upper earnings limit which is £805 per week in 2014/15. Contributions are paid at 2% of earnings above the upper earnings limit. If a person earns less than the primary threshold they will not pay NI contributions. The year will still count towards building up a basic state pension provided the earnings are not less than the lower earnings limit. This is £111 at 2014/15.

Class 2 contributions

Self-employed people will build up their NI contributions by paying class 2 contributions. These are paid either by direct debit or by quarterly bill at the rate of £2.75 per week (2014/15).

If profits are below the 'small earnings exception' which is £5885 in 2014/15 then there is a choice of whether or not to pay NI contributions. However, if this option is chosen, then a state pension will not be building up and there could be a loss of other benefits, such as sickness, bereavement and incapacity.

If you are a director of your own company then class 1 contributions will be paid and not class 2.

Class 3 contributions

If a person is not paying class 1 or 2 contributions or receiving HRP they can pay class 3 voluntary contributions. These are charged at a flat rate of £13.90 per week (2014/15). They can be paid up to 6 years back to make up any shortfall.

National Insurance Credits

In some situations you may get National Insurance Credits, which plug what would otherwise be gaps in your NI record. You might get credits in the following situations.

- when you are unemployed, or unable to work because you are ill, and claiming certain benefits
- If you were aged 16 to 18 before 6 April 2010, you were usually credited automatically with National Insurance credits. No new awards will be made from 6 April 2010.

- if you are on an approved training course
- when you are doing jury service
- if you are getting Statutory Adoption Pay, Statutory Maternity Pay, Additional Statutory Paternity Pay, Statutory Sick Pay, Maternity Allowance or Working Tax Credit
- if you have been wrongly put in prison
- if you are caring for a child or for someone who is sick or disabled
- if you are aged 16 or over and provided care for a child under 12, that you are related to and you lived in the UK for the period(s) of care
- if your spouse or civil partner is a member of Her Majesty's forces and you are accompanying them on an assignment outside the UK

There are special arrangements for people who worked or were detained without pay in Iraq during the Gulf Crisis.

If you think you might be affected by this, write to HM Revenue & Customs (HMRC) at:

HM Revenue & Customs
National Insurance Contributions & Employer Office
Benton Park View
Newcastle upon Tyne
NE98 1ZZ
0300 200 3211

Women's state pension age is gradually increasing and when it matches the State Pension Age for men from April 2020 onwards, this type of credit will no longer be available.

The State Pension age

Currently, the state pension age is 65 for men. On 6th April 2010, the state pension age for women started to increase gradually from 60-65, to match men's. There will be further increases in the state pension age to 68 for men and women. The increase in the State Pension age is being phased in and your own particular pension age depends on when you were born. The proposed changes affect people born between April 1953 and 5th April 1960. The tables below shows the proposed retirement ages. These changes are not yet law as they need to go to parliament for approval. (For your own retirement age you should go to the Pensions Service Website).

Table 1. State pension age if woman born on or after April 6th 1950 but before April 1953

Date of Birth	Date State pension Age Reached
6th April 1951 to 5th May 1951	6th May 2012
6th May 1951 to 5th June 1951	6th July 2012
6th June 1951 to 5th July 1951	6th September 2012
6th July 1951 to 5th August 1951	6th November 2012
6th August 1951 to 5th September 1951	6th January 2013
6th September 1951 to 5th October 1951	6th March 2013
6th October 1951 to 5th November 1951	6th May 2013
6th November 1951 to 5th December 1951	6th July 2013
6th December 1951 to 5th January 1952	6th September 2013
6th January 1952 to 5th February 1952	6th November 2013
6th February 1952 to 5th March 1952	6th January 2014
6th March1952 to 5th April 1952	6th March 2014
6th April1952 to 5th May 1952	6th May 2014
6th May 1952 to 5th June 1952	6th July 2014
6th June 1952 to 5th July 1952	6th September 2014
6th July 1952 to 5th August 1952	6th November 2014
6th August 1952 to 5th September	6th January 2015

1952	
6th September 1952 to 5th October 1952	6th March 2015
6th October 1952 to 5th November 1952	6th May 2015
6th November 1952 to 5th December 1952	6th July 2015
6th December 1952 5th January 1953	6th September 2015
6th January 1953 to 5th February 1953	6th November 2015
6th February 1953to March 1953	6th January 2016
6th March 1953 to 5th April 1953	6th March 2016

Table 2. Your state pension age if you are a woman and you were born on or after 6th April 1953 but before 6th December 1953.

Date you were born	Date you will reach pension age if you are a woman or the pension credit qualifying age for men and women
6th April 1953 to 5th May 1953	6th July 2016
6th May 1953 to 5th June 1953	6th November 2016
6th June 1953 to 5th July 1953	6th March 2017
6th July 1953 to 5th August 1953	6th July 2017
6th August 1953 to 5th September 1953	6th November 2017
6th September 1953 to 5th October 1953	6th March 2018
6th October 1953 to 5th November 1953	6th July 2018
6th November 1053 to 5th December 1953	6th November 2018

Table 3: Your state pension age if you are a man or a woman and you were born on or after 6th December 1953 or before 6th April 1968.

Date you were born	Date you will reach pension age if you are a woman or the pension credit qualifying age for men and women
6th December 1953 to 5th January	6th March 2019

1954	
6th January 1954 to 5th February 1954	6th May 2019
6th February 1954 to 5th March 1954	6th July 2019
6th March 1954 5th April 1954	6th September 2019
6th April 1954 to 5th May 1954	6th November 2019
6th May 1954 to 5th June 1954	6th January 2020
6th June 1954 to 5th July 1954	6th March 2020
6th July 1954 to 5th August 1954	6th May 2020
6th August 1954 to 5th September 1954	6th July 2020
6th September 1954 to 5th October 1954	6th September 2020
6th October 1954 to 5th April 1968	66th birthday

Table 4. Your state pension age if you are a man or woman and you were born on or after 6th April 1968.

Increase from 66 to 67	
Date you were born	Date you will reach pension age if you are a woman or the pension credit qualifying age for men and women
6th April 1968 to 5th May 1968	6th May 2034
6th May 1968 to 5th June 1968	6th July 2034
6th June 1968 to 5th July 1968	6th September 2034
6th July 1968 to 5th August 1968	6th November 2034
6th August 1968 to 5th September 1968	6th January 2035
6th September 1968 to 5th October 1968	6th March 2035
6th October 1968 to 5th November 1968	6th May 2035
6th November 1968 to 5th December 1968	6th July 2035
6th December 1968 to 5th January 1969	6th September 2035
6th January 1969 to 5th February 1969	6th November 2035
6th February 1969 to 5th March 1969	6th January 2036

6th March 1969 to 5th April 1969	6th March 2036
6th April 1969 to 5th April 1977	67th birthday

Table 5. Your State pension age if you are a man or woman and you were born on or after 6th April 1968.

Increase from 67 to 68	
Date you were born	Date you will reach pension age if you are a woman or the pension credit qualifying age for men and women
6th April 1977 to 5th May 1977	6th May 2044
6th May 1977 to 5th June 1977	6th July 2044
6th June 1977 to 5th July 1977	6th September 2044
6th July 1977 to 5th August 1977	6th November 2044
6th August 1977 to 5th September 1977	6th January 2045
6th September 1977 to 5th October 1977	6th March 2045
6th October 1977 to 5th November 1977	6th May 2045
6th November 1977 to 5th December 1977	6th July 2045
6th December 1977 to 5th January 1978	6th September 2045
6th January 1978 to 5th February 1978	6th November 2045
6th February 1978 to 5th March 1978	6th January 2046
6th March1978 to 5th April 1978	6th March 2046
6th April 1978 onwards	68th birthday

State pensions for people over 80

From the age of 80, all pensioners qualify for an extra 25pence per week If a person does not qualify for a basic state pension or is on a low income then they may be entitled to receive what is called ' an over-80's pension' from the age of 80. For further advice concerning pensions either go to the government website www.thepensionsservice.gov.uk or refer to the list of useful leaflets at the back of this book.

Additional state pension

S2P replaced the State Earnings Related Pension (SERPS) in April 2002. SERPS was, essentially, a state second tier pension and it was compulsory to pay into this in order to supplement the basic state pension. There were drawbacks however, and many people fell through the net so S2P was introduced to allow other groups to contribute. S2P refined SERPS allowing the following to contribute:

- People caring for children under six and entitled to child benefit
- Carers looking after someone who is elderly or disabled, if they are entitled to carers allowance
- Certain people who are unable to work because of illness or disability, if they are entitled to long-term incapacity benefit or severe disablement allowance and they have been in the workforce for at least one-tenth of their working life

Self-employed people are excluded from S2P as are employees earning less than the lower earnings limit. Married women and widows paying class 1 contributions at the reduced rate do not build up additional state pension.

S2P is an earnings related scheme. This means that people on high earnings build up more pension than those on lower earnings. However, people earning at least the lower earnings limit (£111) in 2014/15 but less than the low earnings threshold (£153) in 2014/15 are treated as if they have earnings at that level and so build up more pension than they otherwise would.

Contracting out

A person does not build up state additional pension during periods when they are contracted out. Contracting out means that a person has opted to join an occupational scheme or a personal pensions scheme or stakeholder pension. While contacted out, a person will pay lower National Insurance Contributions on part of earnings or some of the contributions paid by an employee and employer are 'rebated' and paid into the occupational pension scheme or other pension scheme. This is discussed more fully further on in this book.

Increasing your state pension

There are a number of ways in which you can increase your State Pension, particularly if you have been presented with a pension forecast which shows lack of contributions and a diminished state pension. You can fill gaps in your pension contributions or you can defer your state pension. HM Revenue and Customs have a help line on 0300 123 1079 to check your record and to receive advice on whether you have gaps and how to fill them.

Filling gaps in your record

For people reaching State Pension Age on, or after, 6th April 2010, you need only 30 qualifying years for the full pension. Depending on your pension age your working life may be from 44 to 52 years. Therefore, under the post April 2010 rules, you can have substantial gaps in your record without any reduction in your basic pension.

If you wish to plug gaps in your contributions, normally you can go back 6 years to fill gaps in your record. However, if you will reach State Pension Age before April 5th 2015, special rules let you fill any gaps up to six years in total going back as far as 6th April 1975. You can make class 3 contributions to fill the gap, each contribution costs £13.90 so a full years worth costs 52 times £13.90 = £722.80 Making class three contributions can't increase your additional state pension. However Class 3 contributions do count towards the state bereavement benefits that your wife, husband or civil partner could claim if you were to die.

Deferring your state pension

Another way to boost your state pension is to delay its commencement. You can put off drawing your pension for as long as you like, there is no time limit. You must defer your whole pension, including any additional or graduated pensions and you earn an addition to the lump sum or a bigger cash sum.

In the past, if you put off drawing your own pension and your wife was getting a pension based on your NI record, her pension would also have to be deferred and she would have to agree to this. From 6th April 2010 onwards, husbands and civil partners as well as wives may be able to claim a pension based on their partners record. But a change to the rules now means that, if you defer your pension and your wife, husband or civil partner claims on your record, they no longer have to defer their pension as well.

If your pension has already started to be paid, you can decide to stop payments in order to earn extra pension or lump sum. But you can only defer your pension once. You can earn an increase in the pension when it does start of 1% for every five weeks you put off the pension. This is equivalent to an increase of 10.4% for each whole year.

Alternatively, if you put off claiming your pension for at least a whole year, you can earn a one-off lump sum instead of extra pension. The lump sum is taxable but only at the top rate you were paying before getting the lump sum. Whatever the size of the sum it does not mean that you move tax brackets.

The Pension Service, which is part of the Department of Work and Pensions publishes a detailed guide to deferring your State pension. Go to www. gov.uk-contact-pension-service.

Changes to the state pension from 2016

From April 2016, the new "flat rate " state pension will typically be £155 a week, but only for those who have paid national insurance contributions (NIC's) for 35 years. Many women will not qualify, having taken career breaks to care for children.

If there are gaps in your entitlement then consider buying some added years of state pension which you can do in the run-up to retirement. The state pension purchase scheme is far more generous than any private pension, provided you live more than a few years in retirement. Be careful, though, that you're not going to be buying years that you'd actually make up through work between now and retirement, otherwise you could end up giving the government money for something you'd have got anyway.

Voluntary NIC's cost £13,90 a week or £722,80 a year, and you can normally fill gaps from the past six years. If you are due to retire after April 2016, check to see how much you will receive at gov.uk/future-pension-centre.

....

17

Job Related Pensions

The best way to save for retirement is through an occupational pension scheme. Employers will also contribute and pay administration costs. Schemes normally provide an additional package of benefits such as protection if you become disabled, protection for dependants and protection against inflation. Some pension schemes are related to final salary and provide a pension that equates to a proportion of salary. However, it must be said that a lot of these schemes are winding down.

Limits on your pension savings

These limits apply collectively to all private pensions (occupational schemes and personal pensions) that you may have)

Type of limit	Description	Amount
Annual contribution limit	The maximum contributions on which you can get tax relief. You can continue contributing to your 75th birthday	£3,600 or 100% of your UK relevant earnings for the year whichever is the greater
Annual allowance	The maximum addition to your pension savings in any one year (including for	Tax year 2014/15 £40,000

	example employers contributions). Anything above the limit normally triggers a tax charge, but this does not apply in the year that you start to draw the pension.	
Lifetime allowance	The cumulative value of benefits that can be drawn from your pension savings. Any amount drawn that exceeds the limits triggers a tax charge.	Tax year 2014/15

Tax advantages of occupational schemes

The tax advantages of occupational schemes are:

- A person receives tax relief on the amount that he or she pays into the scheme
- Employers contributions count as a tax-free benefit
- Capital gains on the contributions build up tax free
- At retirement part of the pension fund can be taken as a tax-free lump sum. The rest is taken as a taxable pension

People aged 65 and over receive more generous tax allowances than younger people. Tax allowances are dealt with further on in the book.

Qualifying to join an occupational scheme

An occupational scheme can be either open to all or restricted to certain groups, i.e. different schemes for different groups. Schemes are not allowed to discriminate in terms of race or gender or any other criteria. Employees do not have to join a scheme and can leave when they wish. There might however be restrictions on rejoining or joining a scheme later on.

Not all employers offer an occupational scheme. Another pension arrangement such as a stakeholder scheme or Group Pension Scheme might be offered.

The amount of pension that a person receives from an occupational scheme will depend in part on the type of scheme that it is. Currently, there are two main types:

- Defined benefit schemes, promising a given level of benefit on retirement, usually final salary schemes
- Money purchase schemes (defined contribution schemes), where a person builds up their own savings pot. There are hybrid schemes where both the above are on offer but these are not common.

Final salary schemes

With final salary schemes, a person is promised (but not guaranteed) a certain level of pension and other benefits related to earnings. This is independent of what is paid into the scheme. Final salary schemes work well when a person stays with their employer for a long length of time or work in the public sector.

A person in such a scheme will typically pay around 5% of their salary into the scheme with the employer paying the balance of the cost which will be around 10% of salary on average. When the stock market is doing well the employer is safeguarded but when the economic climate is changing, such as at this point in time then the story is somewhat different and the employer has to pay more to maintain the level of pension. This is why such pension schemes are being withdrawn.

The pension received at retirement is based on a formula and related to final salary and years of membership in the scheme. The maximum usually builds up over 40 years. The accrual rate in such a scheme is one sixtieth or one eightieth of salary per year in the scheme.

If a person leaves the pension scheme before retirement they are still entitled to receive a pension from the scheme, based on contributions.

'Final salary' defined

The final salary is defined in the rules of the scheme. It can have a variety of meanings, for example average pay over a number of years, average of the best salary for a number of years out of ten, or earnings on a specified date. What counts are the pensionable earnings, which may mean basic salary, or could include other elements such as overtime, bonus etc.

A lump sum tax-free is included in the scheme which is defined by HMRC rules. The lump sum after 40 years of service will be around 1.5 times the annual salary.

Money purchase schemes

Money purchase pension schemes are like any other forms of savings or investment. Money is paid in and grows in value and the proceeds eventually provide a pension. The scheme is straightforward and has its upsides and downsides. The upside is that it is simple and portable. The downside is that it is related to the growth of the economy and can shrink as well as grow.

It is more difficult to plan for retirement with this kind of scheme, as distinct from the final salary scheme. As we have seen, employers prefer this kind of scheme because, although they pay into it, it doesn't place any onerous responsibilities on them.

The pension that is received on retirement will depend on the amount paid into the scheme, charges deducted for management of the scheme, how well the investment grows and the rate, called the annuity rate, at which the fund can be converted into pension. A major problem for pension schemes has been the decline in annuity rates in recent years. With most money purchase schemes the proceeds are usually given to an insurer who will administer the funds. The trustees of the scheme will choose the insurer, in most cases. In some cases, contributors are given the choice of investment. This choice will usually include:

- A with-profits basis which is a medium-risk option and which is safer and more likely to provide a good return if a person remains with the same employer. The value of the fund cannot fall and will grow steadily as reversionary bonuses are added. On retirement a person will receive a terminal bonus, which represents a chunk of the overall return
- A unit linked fund- where money is invested in one or more funds, e.g. shares, property, gilts and so on.

The cash balance scheme

A cash balance scheme lies somewhere between a final salary scheme and a money purchase scheme. Whereas in a final salary scheme a person is promised a certain level of pension at retirement with a cash balance scheme a person is promised a certain amount of money with which to buy a pension. The amount of cash can be expressed in a number of ways, for example as a percentage of salary per annum for each year of membership. So if a person is earning £50,000 per annum and the cash balance scheme is promising 15% of salary for each year of membership, there would be a pension fund of £50,000 times 15% which equals £75,000 after 10 years of membership.

Tax

Whichever type of pension that is offered, the government sets limits on maximum amounts that a person can receive. HMRC sets limits on occupational schemes which relate mainly to final salary schemes and which are shown below.

Main HMRC limits on pensions.

1. If you are in a scheme set up on or after 14th March 1989 or a scheme set up before 14th March 1989 but you joined on or after 1st June 1989, or are in a scheme set up before 14th March 1989 which you joined on or after 17th March 1987 but before 1st June 1989 if you elected to be treated under the 'post 1989 regime'.

Under the above rules you will get a percentage of final salary up to £68,000 with a limit on the lump sum at retirement of 1.5 times final salary up to a maximum of £150,000. These are the limits for the current tax year.

2. If you are in a scheme set up before 14th March 1989 which was joined on or after 17th March 1987 and before 1st June 1989 you will receive a percentage of final salary up to a maximum of 1.5 times salary or £150,000.

If you joined a scheme before 17th March 1987 you will receive a percentage of final salary up to 1.5 times salary.

Normally, the maximum pension and any other benefits build up over a long period, usually 40 years. The pension builds up at a rate of one sixtieth of final salary for each year that you are with the employer. The maximum lump sum builds up at a rate of three-eightieths of final salary.

The rules allow for a faster build up of pension if a person can't build up pension over such a long period.

The pension scheme will set a pension age, and although there used to be difference in the age at which pension was paid to men and women respectively, the dates are now usually harmonised. The most popular age for receiving pension is 65 although some opt for 60. The lowest age at which pensions can be paid is 55. In most cases, a person must give up a job before receiving an occupational pension from an employer. The rules are in the process of changing so that a pension can be received from an employer whilst still working for that employer.

Tax rules set a limit on the amount that a pension can be increased each year. This is usually inflation. If the starting pension is less than the Inland Revenue maximum then bigger increases are allowed. For pensions built up from April 6th 1997 onwards the increase is limited to a limited price indexation which means that each year the pension can be increased in line with inflation up to a maximum of 2.5% per year.

Contributions into occupational schemes

Some occupational schemes are non-contributory, which means that the employer pays all contributions. The majority of schemes, however, are contributory, with the employer and employee contributing. Usually, the employee will pay 5% of salary. With money purchase schemes the employer will also pay a specified amount of salary. With final salary schemes, which as stated are becoming less and less common, the employer will make up the balance needed to provide the specified amount. Both employer and employee will get tax relief on contributions.

Top-up schemes exist which can be used to top up pension pots but these are liable for tax in the usual way. There are two main types of top-up scheme:

- Unfunded schemes. With these schemes, an employer simply pays benefits at the time that a person reaches retirement. Income tax will be due on any benefits, even on lump sums
- funded schemes (Funded Unapproved Retirement Benefit Schemes or FURBS). This is where the employer pays contributions which build up funds to provide the eventual benefits. At the time that contributions are made they count as tax-liable fringe benefits. Usually the fund is arranged as a trust, which attracts only normal rates of tax. The benefits are tax-free when they are paid out, having been subject to tax.

If an employer runs a scheme which a person is eligible to join they must be given information about it automatically. The rules are as follows:

- an explanatory booklet must be given within two months of commencing employment if eligible to join, or within 13 weeks of joining
- each year a summary trustees report an annual accounts must be given

- employees can request a copy of the full accounts which must be provided on request
- an annual benefit statement must be provided
- options on leaving the scheme and benefit entitlements, transfer value must be provided within 3 months of request
- any announcements of changes to the scheme must be given to the scheme member within one month of the change being made

....

18

Group Personal Pension Schemes

Group personal pension schemes are a popular alternative to occupational pension schemes, particularly to smaller employers.

Group personal pension schemes are not occupational pension schemes. They are pension schemes tailored to employees of a company. The employer is not obliged to pay anything into such schemes, although many do. The amount an employer will pay is often less than an occupational pension scheme. The employee will usually end up contributing more.

Group personal pension schemes work on a money purchase basis, and, as we have seen, the employee will bear all the risks themselves. The administration charges for group personal pension schemes are usually the same as other pension funds. A plus side of group schemes is that they are seen to be particularly suitable for employees on short term contracts who cannot build up reasonable benefits in an occupational scheme because of frequent job changes. Group pension schemes are personal and travel with the employee and can be kept going without a break.

Group Personal pension Schemes and stakeholder schemes

Since October 2001, employers with more than five employees must offer at least an occupational pension scheme, a group scheme or a stakeholder scheme to employees. Stakeholder schemes are outlined further on in the book.

The pension on retirement from a group scheme will depend on the same factors as all money purchase schemes, such as the overall amount paid in and the performance of the investment. In addition, the charges taken to administer the scheme will influence the amount left in the pot.

In terms of receipt of a tax-free lump sum, group schemes are exactly the same as all other pension funds.

****

19

New Duties for Employers Relating to Provision of Pensions from 2012

From 2012, changes to pensions law affected all employers with at least one worker in the UK.

Employers need to:

- Automatically enrol certain workers into a pension scheme
- Make contributions on their workers behalf
- Register with the Pensions Regulator
- Provide workers with information about the changes and how they will affect them.

The new employer duties were introduced in stages over 4 years, starting in 2012. Each employer will be allocated a date from when the duties will first apply to them, know as their 'staging date'. This date is based on the number of people in an employer's PAYE scheme. Employers with the largest number of employee's in their PAYE scheme will have the earliest staging date. These staging dates can be checked on www.tpr.gov.uk/staging.

Automatic enrolment

Workers who need to be automatically enrolled are called' eligible jobholders'. An eligible jobholder is:

- Aged between 22 and the state pension age
- Working, or ordinarily working in the UK
- Earning above a certain amount (currently £10,000).

The location of the employer is not relevant when considering if the worker is an eligible jobholder. Neither is the worker's nationality or the length of their stay in the UK.

When considering whether a workers earnings are above or below the lower earnings limit, an employer needs to look at what is known as the workers 'qualifying earnings'. This will include earnings in salary, overtime, commission, bonuses, sick pay, maternity, paternity and adoption pay.

Choosing a pension scheme

Employers with an automatic enrolment duty will need to choose a pension scheme they can use for automatic enrolment. Information from the Pensions Regulator will be available to help inform this decision. Employers might use an existing scheme or set up a new one with a pension provider.

In addition, there is the National Employment Savings Trust (NEST). NEST is a pension scheme with the following characteristics:

- It has a public service obligation, meaning it must accept all employers who apply.
- It has been established by government to ensure that employers, including those that employ low to medium earners, can access pension savings and comply with their automatic enrolment duties.

Whether the scheme an employer uses for automatic enrolment is new or not, it must meet certain specific set out in legislation.

The scheme cannot:

- Impose barriers, such as probationary periods or age limits for workers.
- Require staff to make an active choice to join or take other action, e.g. having to sign a form or provide extra information to the scheme themselves, either prior to joining or to retain active membership of the scheme.

Each pension scheme will have its own rules, but all employers will need to provide the scheme with certain information about the person who is automatically enrolled.

Employers/employee contributions

Many employers offer a defined contribution scheme to staff. The rules of these schemes must require the employer to pay an overall minimum contribution of at least 8% of the workers qualifying earnings, of which at least 3% must be from the employer. In most cases, government tax relief will account for 1% of the total 8%. Employers who already have a pension scheme can confirm that it is suitable for automatic enrolment by a process called 'certification'.

Opt-out

Workers who have been automatically enrolled have the right to opt out of the employer's pension scheme by effectively giving one months notice. To opt out, workers must give notice via an 'opt out' notice to the employer. When employers receive a valid opt out notice within the 1-month period, they must pay back any contributions deducted from the workers pay.

Other workers
As well as automatically enrolling eligible jobholders, employers must also put certain other workers into a pension scheme, if these

individuals ask. More information will be available from the Pensions Regulator later this year. Their website is www.thepensionsregulator.gov.uk.

....

20

Protecting Pensions

It is not surprising that people get very disillusioned and nervous when it comes to pensions. Since the 1980's there have been a number of scandals involving blatant theft of pensions and also incidences of mis-selling.

During the 1950's, one of Britain's biggest insurance companies, Equitable life, offered pensions which were supposed to guarantee a fixed level of income at retirement. However, by the 1990's these guarantees became too expensive and the company could not fulfill their promises. Equitable life faced many legal challenges and stopped taking on any new business. Many pensioners found themselves with poor returns and it is only now that the government is looking at compensating the victims.

In addition to theft and bad management the usual raft of 'financial advisors' mis-sold personal pensions, taking advantage particularly of the changes in the 1980's and peoples confusion. Although many people received compensation, many others did not and a lot of distress was caused to a lot of people.

To add to the above a lot of companies became insolvent and there was too little in the pension funds to fulfill pension promises. In the early days (early 2000's) there was a spate of these insolvencies and lots of people lost their pension or received less than they had planned for. The government set up several schemes to help such people and a compensation scheme was set up to assist.

The main risk to pension funds lies with occupational schemes. Although people need to be aware of changes to the state pension scheme it is safe in so far as the state is unlikely to become insolvent and unable to pay. For sure people need to keep abreast of legislation and changes to state pensions but in essence the amount promised will remain safe.

Occupational schemes

As discussed above, one of the main risks to occupational pensions is that the employer might embezzle the funds. This should be difficult given the role of the pension trustees, which will be outlined below, but it is always possible. There is also the risk that the scheme cannot pay the amount promised. This can be to do with stock market fluctuations, or, as we have all painfully seen in the last few years, a deep recession which affects people and pensions globally.

Another problem that may arise is that of schemes with defined benefits, final salary schemes, changing their rules and replacing defined benefits with less generous schemes.

Protecting pensions

Occupational schemes are usually either statutory schemes or are set up under a trust. A statutory scheme is as the name implies. It is set up under an Act of Parliament and is the usual arrangement for most public sector schemes such as police, NHS, teachers and so on. Private sector schemes are usually always set up under a trust. This ensures that the scheme is kept at arms length from the employer and business, and can't go down with the sinking ship. (Many lessons have been learned post-Mirror Group and Robert Maxwell). With a trust you will have three main elements:

- The sponsor, who will be the employer, who will initially decide on the rules of the scheme along with the benefits
- the beneficiaries, who are scheme members and any beneficiaries who might benefit if, say, a scheme member passes away
- Very importantly, the trustees who are tasked with looking after the pension fund and making sure that it is administered in accordance with the scheme rules.

The trustees are responsible for the running of the scheme but can also employ outside help, specialist help and can employ someone to administrate the scheme. They are supported in this role by the Pensions Regulator, which is the official body that regulates all worked based schemes (occupational schemes and also those personal pensions and stakeholder schemes organized through the workplace). The Pensions Regulator promotes good practice, monitors risk, investigates schemes and responds to complaints from scheme members. The Pensions Regulator has many powers, as would be expected, and can prosecute those who it thinks guilty of wrongdoing.

There is a Fraud Compensation Fund which can pay out where an occupational pension schemes assets have been embezzled or reduced because of dishonest activity. The fund is financed by a levy on all occupational pension schemes.

Other schemes
Normally, if there is a shortfall when a pension scheme is wound up, the employer would be expected to make up any shortfall. However, clearly this is not possible if the employer is insolvent and there is no money to put into a scheme. Between 1997 and 2005 some 85,000 people lost some or all of their promised pensions because of insolvency.

Because of this several schemes were set up to provide protection:

- Financial Assistance Scheme (FAS). This scheme was set up and funded by the government to provide help for those pensions scheme members in greatest need where their pension scheme started to wind up between 1st January 1997 to 5th April 2005. This is administered by the Pensions Regulator.

- Pension Protection Fund (PPF). This scheme took over from the above to provide compensation where a scheme winds up on or after 6th April 2005 with too little in the fund or an insolvent employer. In general, compensation ensures that existing pensioners carry on getting the full amount of their pension and that other scheme members get 90% of their promised pension up to a maximum limit (£36,401 at 65 in 2014-15). The PPF is financed by a levy on occupational pension schemes.

- For full details of the Pension protection fund you should go to www.pensionprotectionfund.org.uk.

Protection of personal pensions

Nearly all personal pensions come under the umbrella of the Financial Conduct Authority (FCA). In the United Kingdom, it is illegal to offer personal pensions without being authorized by the FCA. All pension providers authorized by then FCA have to go through a lot of hoops to demonstrate that they are responsible providers. The FCA oversees the activities of the Financial Services Compensation Scheme.

If a firm providing personal pensions becomes insolvent the FSCS will step in and provide compensation instead. Compensation is capped at a maximum amount, which varies according to the way that your money has been invested. Currently the maximum is

£50,000 for deposits, £50,000 for investments and for long term insurance (personal pensions, life insurance and annuities 90% of the claim with no upper limit).

Complaining about pensions
State pensions

In the first instance you would deal with HMRC, regarding payment of national insurance, and also the Pension Service regarding pension forecasts. You can find details about how to complain from HMRC website www.hmrc.gov.uk. If you have complained to the director of a particular office and you are not happy you can take your complaint to the Adjudicators Office (www.adjudicatorsoffice.gov.uk). This is an independent body that can deal with complaints about mistakes and delays, misleading advice and any other issue. In the same way you should contact the Pensions Service department dealing with pension forecasts if you have a problem in this area. If the problem carries on without resolution you can contact the Pensions Service Chief Executive.

Occupational schemes

You should initially contact the pension administrator for your scheme. If the problem is not resolved at this early stage then you should say that you want to use the formal complaints procedure, which all occupational schemes must have and must provide you with details of. If you receive no satisfaction with this process then you should contact the Pensions Advisory Service (TPAS) www.pensionsadvisoryservice.org.uk.

TPAS is an independent mediation service which will help all parties reach agreement. If this doesn't work then you can go one step further and take your complaint to the Pensions Ombudsman. You must go through TPAS before the Ombudsman will consider your complaint.

Personal pensions

You should complain first to the pensions provider. As mentioned, all firms authorized by the FSA must have a formal complaints procedure. Provided that you go down this route, and you are still unhappy, then you can complain to the Financial Ombudsman Service (FOS) www.financial-ombudsman.org.uk. It will investigate your complaint and can make orders which are binding on the firm. Where appropriate the FOS can make the firm pay you up to £100,000 to put the matter right.

....

21

Tax and Pensions

State pensions

State retirement pensions count as income for tax purposes. Tax may have to be paid if income received is high enough. The only exception to this is the £10 Christmas bonus paid to all pensioners.

State pension is paid without deduction of tax. This is convenient for non-taxpayers. For other taxpayers, the tax due will usually be deducted from PAYE or from any other pension that is received. If the tax is not deducted it will be collected through self-assessment in January and July instalments.

Occupational schemes

A pension from an occupational scheme is treated as income for tax purposes. Usually, the pension will be paid with tax deducted through the PAYE system, along with any other tax due.

Personal pensions

A personal pension will count as income for tax purposes. The pension provider will usually deduct tax through PAYE. Likewise, any other tax due will be deducted through the PAYE system. The local tax office should be contacted in order to determine individual tax positions.

Tax in retirement

When a person retires, their tax bill continues to be worked out in the usual way. However, higher tax allowances may apply so less tax is paid.

The calculations used to work out a person's individual tax bill are as follows:

- Income from all sources is added together. This includes all income with the exception of income that is tax-free.
- Outgoings that you pay in full are deducted from taxable income. 'Outgoings' means any expenditure that qualifies for tax relief.
- Allowances are subtracted. Everyone has a personal allowance. For current allowances, contact the local HMRC Office or Citizens Advice Bureau. There is a breakdown below
- What is left is taxable income. This divided into four. The first slice tax is paid at the basic rate of 20% (0-£31865) the second slice £31866-£150,000 is subject to 40% tax. The third slice is over £150,000 subject to 45% tax. (as at 2014/2015)
- Married couples allowance-this is a reduced rate allowance, given at a rate of 10% as a reduction to a person's tax bill. Married couples allowance is given only where a husband or wife were born before 6th April 1935.

Tax allowances for retirees

In the tax year 2014/15 the basic personal allowance for most people is £10,000. However, if a person is 65 or over at any time during a tax year, there will be a higher personal allowance, the age-allowance. There are two rates of age allowance: in the 2014/15 tax year the allowance is £10,500 for people reaching ages 65 to 74, and the higher age allowance is £10660 for people reaching ages 75 or more. A husband and wife can each get a personal allowance to set against their own income. See table below

Born between 6 April 1938 and 5 April 1948

Income	Personal Allowance
£0 to £26,999	£10,500
£27,000 to £27,999	Between £10,500 and £10,000. Your allowance (£10,500) goes down by £1 for every £2 that your adjusted net income's over £27,000.
£28,000 to £100,000	£10,000

Born before 6 April 1938

Income	Personal Allowance
£0 to £26,999	£10,660
£27,000 to £28,319	Between £10,660 and £10,000. Your allowance (£10,660) goes down by £1 for every £2 that your adjusted net income's over £27,000.
£28,320 to £100,000	£10,000

There is an extra allowance called a married couples allowance if you are married or in a civil partnership and either husband or wife, or both, were born before 6th April 1935. While the personal allowance saves tax at the highest rate, the married couples allowance only gives tax relief at the rate of 10% in the 2014/ 15tax year. If the husbands income is above a certain level then the married couples allowance is reduced, but never to less than a basic amount. A wife can elect to have half the basic amount of the married couples allowance (but not any of the age-related addition) set against her own income. Alternatively, the husband and wife can elect jointly for the whole basic amount to be transferred to the wife. If both partners were born after 1935, you may be able to claim marriage allowance instead. For more details go to www.gov.uk-marriage-allowance.

....

22

Reaching Retirement Age

On reaching retirement age, it will be necessary to ensure that all paperwork relating to pension contributions is in order. There are a number of rules that should be observed in order to ensure that any pension due is paid:

- keep all documents relating to pension rights
- start organising any pension due before retirement, this will ensure that any problems are overcome well before retirement

It is very important that communication is kept with all pension providers, and that they have accurate up-to-date records of a person's whereabouts. Each time addresses are changed this should be communicated to all pension providers. If it is impossible to track down an old employer from whom a pension is due, the Pension Schemes Registry can help. The Pensions Regulator is responsible for the Pension Schemes Registry. This was set up in 1990, by the government to help people trace so-called 'lost pensions'. If help is needed this can be obtained by filling in a form which can be accessed on the website of the pensions regulator www.pensionsregulator.gov.uk

How to claim state pension

A letter will be sent to all retiree's about four months before retirement date. This will come from the pension service and will detail how much pension is due. The pension is not paid automatically, it has to be claimed. This can be done by phoning the Pensions Claim Line number included with the letter, or by filling in a claim form BR1. If the person is a married man and the wife is claiming based on the husbands contributions, then form BF225 should be filled in. If the pension is to be deferred it is advisable to contact the Pensions Service in writing as soon as possible at www. pensionsadvisoryservice.org.uk. A late pension claim can be backdated up to twelve months. If a man is claiming for a pension for his wife based on his contributions this can only be backdated six-months.

How the pension is paid

Pensions are paid by the DWP pension direct to a bank account or Post Office Card Account. To find out more about the payment of pensions contact the DWP www.dwp.gov.uk

Leaving the country

If a person goes abroad for less than six months, they can carry on receiving pension in the normal way. If the trip is for longer then the Pension Service should be contacted and one of the following arrangements can be made to pay a pension:

- Have it paid into a personal bank account while away
- Arrange for it to be paid into a Post Office Card Account
- Arrange for the money to be paid abroad
- If a person is living outside of the UK at the time of the annual pension increase they won't qualify for the increase unless they reside in a member country of the European Union or a country with which the UK has an agreement for increasing pensions. It is very important that you check what will happen to your state pension when you move abroad. The DWP International Pension Centre can help

- on 0191 218 7777, or access advice through their main website.

Pensions from an occupational scheme

Although different schemes have different arrangements, there are similar rules for each scheme. About three months before a person reaches normal retirement age, they should contact the scheme. Either telephone or write enclosing all the details that they will need. The following questions should be asked:

- What pension is due?
- What is the lump-sum entitlement?
- How will the pension be reduced if a lump sum is taken?
- How will the pension be paid, will there be any choices as to frequency?
- Is there a widow's or widowers pension, and if so how will it affect the retirement pension?
- Are there any pensions for other dependants in the event of death?

If a person has been making Additional Voluntary Contributions, then a detailed breakdown of these will be needed.

Retiring early

Retirement earlier than the normal age for a scheme may result in payment of a pension at an earlier age. The minimum age for a pension is 55 with the exception of retirement on ill-health grounds. A scheme administrator will be able to supply full details.

Retiring late

Depending on the rules of the occupational scheme it may be possible to delay retirement and take the pension later. Again, the scheme administrators can help.

Method of payment

Depending on how the pension is arranged, it may be paid direct from the provider or via an insurance company. The usual for pension payments is either quarterly or monthly in advance into a personal bank account. The scheme administrators will be able to provide more information with regard to this.

A pension from a personal plan

In the same way as a pension from an occupational scheme, it is necessary to get in touch with the pension provider about 3-4 months before retirement date. The main questions that should be asked are:

- How much is the pension fund worth?
- How much pension will the plan provider offer?
- Can an increase be arranged each year and if so how much is the increase?
- What is the maximum lump sum?
- Is there a widow's or widowers or other dependants pension?
- What are the other options if any?
- Can the purchase of an annuity be deferred without affecting the drawing of an income?

Pensions can only be paid by an insurance company or a friendly society so if the pension has been with any other form of provider then it has to be switched before it can be paid.

If there are protected-rights from a contracted out pension plan, these can be, may have to be, treated quite separately from the rest of a pension. Protected rights from a personal pension cannot be paid until a person has reached 60 years of age. A person must, by law, have an open market option enabling protected rights pension to be paid by another provider, if it is desired.

Choosing the right annuity

It is very important that an open market option is exercised at retirement. Advice should be obtained from a specialist annuity advisor. If husband and wife, it may be advisable to take out a joint annuity which will carry on paying out an income until the last partner dies, otherwise a widower or widow could be left in financial hardship. One popular option is an annuity that pays a guaranteed income for five-years. The usual annuity pays a lifetime income then stops on death. Another option is to take out an increasing annuity. This is compulsory for contracted-out pension rights, but otherwise optional.

As annuities have fallen over the years, another option is to take out a with-profits annuity. This is a higher risk option but offers a higher return. Income from a with-profits annuity is usually made up of two parts: a guaranteed basic payment and bonuses. At the time of taking out the annuity a person must choose the starting income which the annuity will provide. The choice will depend on the likely level of future bonuses (assumed bonuses ABR) and the degree of risk that can be borne. There is a choice between:

- Low ABR (minimum 0% or no bonuses). The annuity income will start at a very low level. But as long as any bonus is declared the income will increase.
- Higher ABR (maximum say 4%). The starting income will be higher. The higher the ABR that is chosen the greater the starting income. Each year, provided the bonus that is declared is greater than the ABR that you chose, the income will increase. If the declared bonus is lower than the ABR, the income will fall back.

Annuity deferral and income withdrawal

Pension plans set up on or after 1st May 1995 can offer the option of annuity deferral and income withdrawal which allows a person to start taking an income from a pension plan but without buying an annuity. Instead, the income is drawn down direct from the pension fund. The remaining fund must be used to buy an annuity before the age of 75. The income must be reviewed every three years to ensure that the pension fund isn't being depleted too fast.

Payments of personal pensions

If the amount involved is very small then this can be taken as a lump sum. The amount is £2,500 or less or is too small to buy a £250 annuity income. Otherwise, the usual arrangements will apply, with you choosing the most convenient method of payment, by cheque, or payment monthly or quarterly into a bank account.

....

23

Continuing to Work

So far, this section has been about taking care to provide for your pension, and also when and how to draw it when the time is right. The time may not be right at the official retirement age. This is very much an individual decision and you have the right to carry on working.

Default retirement age

The default retirement age has been abolished. Before, the employer had the right to make you retire at the age of 65. However, now, if you did not receive notification of your retirement from your employer before 6th April 2011, the default retirement age will not apply to you. If your employer did not notify you of your retirement age before 6th April 2011, they can still decide at what age you retire but the reasons have to be justified to an Employment Tribunal if the decision is questioned.

Changing your job

There is nothing to stop you drawing a pension from one employer's scheme and then taking up employment elsewhere. The age discrimination rules apply to recruitment and so place a general ban on turning down an applicant on the basis of age. However, there are various exceptions. You can be turned down legally because of age if you are older than 65 (or the employers normal retirement age if younger) or you are within six months of reaching that age. If there are objective grounds for turning you down then the employer can do so. One such ground is that you may not be able to work for a reasonably long enough period after training.

Finally, if there is a genuine occupational reason for turning you down such as needing a younger person to act in a role.

Running your own business

Retirement can be an opportunity to start your own business, perhaps turning a hobby into a business or trying something else completely new. This could be pursuing a dream, such as buying and selling property, self-publishing or whatever you have been developing or thinking about but didn't have the time to do when you were working.

Choosing the right business for you is not just a matter of thinking about the skills that you have. You should give serious thought to the work/life balance that you want to create. Some business take up a lot of time and can create a lot of stress, such as purchasing a shop. This in particular is likely to dominate your time and should, realistically, be avoided, unless you are absolutely certain about what you want to sell and where.

Business structure and tax

One of the first decisions is whether to set up a company, work in a partnership or go self-employed. By far the easiest route is to be self-employed. There are no formalities, such as setting up a company. You simply start trading, although you must register your business with HM Revenue and Customs within three months of the end of the month in which you start trading. You will have to fill in a tax return after the end of each tax year. Any profit that you make is added to your other income-such as pensions and any taxable investment income-to see if the total is high enough for you to have to pay tax.

Partnerships

From a tax point of view, partnerships are treated the same way as being self-employed. As with being self-employed, you have three months to register that you have started up and must complete an annual tax return. You should always try to have a formal agreement with any partners and get a solicitor to draw it up.

Trading as a company

This is the most top-heavy way of trading and there are a number of formalities to go through. These include forming a company, choosing a name and registering the company with Companies House who will require you to send in an annual return and also accounts each year. You will also need to contact your local tax office to tell them that you have started trading. By far and away the simplest form of business structure is that of self-employed and you should go this route if possible.

USEFUL ORGANISATIONS

MANAGING MONEY

Association of Investment
Trust Companies (AITC)
23rd floor Durrant House
8-13 Chiswell Street
London EC1Y 4YY
Tel: 020 7285 5555
www.aitc.co.uk

Debt Management Office
Eastcheap Court
11 Philpot Lane
London EC3M 8UD
Tel: 0845 357 6500
www.dmo.gov.uk

Department for Work and Pensions (DWP)
If you ring The Pension Service on 0845 606 0265,
You will be connected to the pension centre covering you area,
Or you can look on the website (www.
Thepensionservice.gov.uk/contact)

Another useful DWP website is www.pensionguide.gov.uk

You can obtain DWP leaflets from Pension Service and
Jobcentre Plus office and some post offices, CABs or
Libraries.

You can write to:

Pension Guides
Freepost
Bristol BS38 7WA
Tel: 08457 31 32 33
If you have access to the Internet, you can download the leaflets
(and claim forms for many of the benefits)
from www.dwp.gov. uk or www.thepensionservice.gov.uk

Disability Alliance
Universal House
88-94 Wentworth Street
London E1 7SA
Tel: 020 7247 8776 www.disabilityalliance.org
Provides advice and publications on social security benefits
For disabled people.

Financial Ombudsman
Service (FOS)
South Quay Plaza
183 Marsh Wall
London E14 9SR
Consumer helpline: 0845 080 1800
www.financialombudsman.org,uk

Financial Conduct Authority (FSA)
25 The North Colonnade
Canary Wharf
London E14 5HS
Consumer helpline: 0845 606 1234
www.fca.gov.uk/consumer

HM Revenue & Customs (HMRC)
The government department that deals

With almost all the taxes due in the UK.
Most HMRC leaflets can be obtained
From local tax offices or Tax Enquiry Centres
(look for in the phone book under `Revenue'
or `Government Department')
or Jobcentre Plus offices.
Almost all are also available on the website at:
www.hmrc.gov.uk or you can ring them the Orderline:
Tel: 0845 900 0404 or write to :
PO Box 37
St Austel
Cornwall PL25 5YN

International Pension Centre
The Pension Service
Tyneview Park
Newcastle upon Tyne NE98 1BA
Tel: 0191 7777
(8.00am-8.00pm,weekdays)

Investment Management Association
65 Kingsway
London WC2B 6TD
Tel: 020 7831 0898
Information line 020 7269 4639
www.investmentfunds.org.uk
(OEIC.S).

MoneyFACTS
MoneyFacts House
66-70 Thorpe Road
Norwich NR1 1BJ
Tel: 0870 2250 476

www.moneyfactsgroup.co.uk

Office of the Public Guardian
Archway Tower
2 Junction Road
London N19 5SZ
Enquiry line: 0845 330 2900
Enduring Powers of Attorney: 0845 330 2963

The Pension Service
State Pension Forecasting Team
Future Pension Centre
Tyneview Park
Whitley Road Newcastle upon Tyne NE98 1BA
Tel: 0845 3000 168 www.thepensionservice.gove.uk

Pension Tracing Service
Tel: 0845 600 2537 www.thepensionservice.gov.uk

Pension Advisory Service
(TPAS)
11 Belgrave Road
London SW1V 1RB
Helpline: 0845 601 2923
www.pensionsadvisoryservice.org.uk

Principal Registry of the Family Division
(HM Courts Service)
First Avenue House
42-49 High Holborn
London WC1V 6NP
Tel: 020 7947 6989 www.courts-service.gov.uk
Wills can be lodged with the Probate Department ;

For a charge of £15. For information about
The leaflet ` I want to deposit my will for safe
Keeping at the Principal Registry of the Family Division'.

Tax Help for Older People
Pineapple Business Park
Salway Ash
Bridport
Dorset DT6 5DB
Tel: 0845 601 3321 www.taxvol.org.uk

KEEPING ACTIVE

Association of British Insurers (ABI)
51 Gresham Street
London EC2V 7HQ
Tel: 020 7600 0713
www.abi.org.uk

Association of British Travel
Agents (ABTA)
68-71 NEWMAN Street
London W1T 3AH
Tel: 020 7637 2444
www.abtanet.com

British Franchise Association
(BFA)
Thames View
Newtown Road
Henley on Thames
Oxon RG9 1HG
Tel: 01491 578050 www.franchisedirect.com

Community Service
Volunteers (CSV)
237 Pentonville Road
London N1 9NJ
Tel: 020 7278 6601
www.cvs.org.uk

Cyclists' Touring Club
(CTC)
Parklands
Railton Road
Guildford
Surrey GU2 9JX
Tel: 0844 736 8451
www.ctc.org.uk

Department for Transport
Mobility and Inclusion Unit
Great Minster House
76 Marsham Street
London SW1P 4DR
Tel: 020 7944 8300

Blue Badge helpline: 020
7944 2914/0161 367 0009
www.dft.gov.uk

Disabled Persons Railcard
Office
PO Box 163
Newcastle upon Tyne
NE12 8WX
Tel:0845 605 0525

www.railcard.co.uk

European Health Insurance
Card (EHIC)
EHIC Enquiries
PO Box 1114
Newcastle upon Tyne NE99
2TL
Tel: 0845 605 0707
www.ehic.org.uk

Forum of Mobility Centres
C/o Providence Chapel
Warehorne
Ashford
Kent TN26 2JX
Tel: 0800 559 3636
(9.00am-5.00pm, weekdays)
www.mobility-centre.org.uk

A network of independent
Mobility centres that offer
Information, advice and
Assessment to people who
Who want to begin, or return to,
Driving after illness, injury or accident.

Learndirect
Tel:0800 150 450
www.learndirect.co.uk
For free advice about all
Areas of learning and
Training.

Tel: 0800 101 901
www.learndirect-advice.co.uk

Mobility
Motability Car Scheme
City Gate House
22 Southwark Bridge Road
London SE1 9HB
Tel: 0300 456 4566
(8.30am- 5.30pm,weekdays)
www.motability.co.uk

National Association of
Councils for Voluntary
And Community Service
(NACVS)
177 Arundel Street
Sheffield S1 2NU
Tel: 0114 278 6636 www.nacvs.org.uk

National Federation of
Women's Institutes (NFWI)
104 New Kings Road
London SW6 4LY
Tel: 020 7371 9300
www.nfwi.org.uk

National Institute of Adult
Continuing Education
(NIACE)
Renaissance House
20 Princess Road West
Leicester LE1 6TP

Tel: 0116 204 4200/4201
www.niace.org.uk

National Trust
PO Box 39
Warrington WA5 7WD
Tel: 0844 800 1895
www.nationaltrust.org.uk

Open University (OU)
PO Box 197
Milton Keynes MK7 6BJ
Tel: 0845 300 6090 www.open.ac.uk

Age UK England
1268 London Road
London SW16 4ER
Helpline: 0800 783 1904
Tel: 020 8765 7200
www.primeinitiative.org.uk

RADAR (Royal Association
For Disability and Rehabilitation)
12 City Forum
250 City Road
London EC1V 8AF
Tel: 020 7250 3222
www.radar.org.uk

Ramblers' Association
2nd Floor
Camelford House
87-90 Albert Embankment

London SE1 7TW
Tel: 020 7339 8500 www.ramblers.org.uk

Retired and Senior Volunteer
Programme (RSVP)
237 Pentonville Road
London N1 9NJ
Tel: 020 7643 1385
www.csv-rsvp.org.uk

The Age Employment
Network (TAEN)
207-221 Pentonville Road
London N1 9UZ
Tel: 020 7843 1590
www.taen.org.uk
Townswoman
1st Floor
329 Tyburn Road
Birmingham B24 8HJ
Tel: 0121 326 0400
www.townswoman.org.uk

Voluntary Service Overseas
(VSO)
317 Putney Bridge Road
London SW15 2PN
Tel: 020 8780 7200
www.vso.org.uk

Volunteering England
Regent's Wharf
8 All Saints Street

London N1 9RL
Tel: 020 77136161
www.volunteeringengland.org.uk

Walking Women
22 Duke Street
Leamington Spa
Warwick CV32 4TR
Tel: 01926 313321
www.walkingwomen.com

Working for a Charity
NCVO
Regent's Wharf
8 All Saints Street
London N1 9RL
Tel:020 7520 2512
www.workingforcharity.org.uk

RUNNING YOUR HOME

Abbeyfield Society
Abbeyfield House
53 Victoria Street
St Albans
Hertfordshire AL1 3UW
Tel: 01727 857536
www.abbeyfield.com

AIMS (Advice Information and
Mediation Service for
Retirement housing)
Astral House

1268 London Road
London SW16 4ER
Advice line: 0845 600 2001
www.ageconcern.org.uk/aims

Almshouse Association
Billingbear Lodge
Maidenhead Road
Wokingham
Berkshire RG40 5RU
Tel: 01344 452922 www.almshouses.org

Pet Travel Scheme(PETS)
Eastbury House
30 –34 Albert Embankment
London SE1 7TL
Helpline: 08459 33 55 77
www.defra.gov.uk/animalh/quarantine

Disabled Living Foundation
(DLF)
380-384 Harrow Road
London W9 2HU
Helpline: 0845 130 9177
Demonstration centre:
0845 130 9177
Tel: 020 7289 6111
www.dlf.org.uk

Elderly Accommodation
Counsel (EAC)
3rd Floor
89 Albert Embankment

London SE1 7TP
Adviceline: 020 7820 1343
www.housingcare.org

Energywatch
Percy House
Percy Street
Newcastle upon Tyne NE1
4PW
Helpline: 0845 906 0708
www.energywatch.org.uk

Federation of Master
Builders (FMB)
Gordon Fisher House
14-15 Great James Street
London WC1N 3DP
Tel: 020 7242 7583
www.fmb.org.uk

Foundations (the national co-ordinating
Body for home improvement agencies)
Bleaklow House
Howard Town Mill
Glossop SK13 8HT
Tel: 01457 891909
www.foundations.uk.com

Trust Mark
Englemere
Kings Ride
Ascot SL5 7TB
Tel:08707 38 48 58 www.trustmark.org.uk

STAYING HEALTHY

Ageing Well UK
Age Concern England
1268 London Road
London SW16 4ER
Information line: 0208 765 7200
www. Ageconcern.org.uk/

Arthritis Care
18 Stephenson Way
London NW1 2HD
Helpline: 0808 800 4050
Tel: 020 7380 6500
www.athritiscare.org.uk

Breast Cancer Care
210 New Kings Road
London SW6 4NZ
Helpline:0207 384 2984
www.breastcancercare.org.ul

British Dental Health
Foundation
Smile House
2 East Union Street
Rugby
Warwickshire CV22 6AJ
Helpline: 0845 063 1188
Tel: 01788 539793
www.dentalhealth.org.uk

Diabetes UK
Macleod House
10 Parkway
London NW1 7AA
Careline: 0845 120 2960
Tel: 020 7424 1000
www.diabetes.org.uk

Hearing Concern
95 Gray's Inn Road
London WC1X 8TX
HelpDesk: 0845 0744 600
(voice & text)
Tel: 020 7440 9871
Textphone:020 7440 9873 {?1}
www.hearingconcern.org.uk

Incontact
SATRA Innovation Park
Rockingham Road
Kettering NN16 9JH
Helpline:0845 257 3540
www.incontact.org

Institute of Trichologists
Ground Floor Office
24 Langroyd Road
London SW17 7PL
Tel: 0870 607 0602
www.trichologists.org.uk

Keep Fit Association
1 Grove House

Foundry Lane
Horsham
West Sussex RH13 5PL
Tel: 01493 266000
Also 0800 808 5252
www.keepfit.org.uk

National Osteoporosis
Society (NOS)
Manor Farm
Skinners Hill Camerton Bath BA2 OPJ
Tel: 01761 471771
Helpline: 0845 450 0230
www.nos.org.uk

NHS DIRECT
Tel:0845 46 47
Nhsdirect.nhs.uk
24- hour telephone and on line advice

NHS Drinkline
Freephone: 0800 917 8282
(9.00am- 11.00pm, weekdays)

Patients Association
PO Box 935
Harrow
Middlesex HA1 3YJ
Helpline: 0845 608 4455
Tel: 020 8423 9111
www.patientsassociation.com

Royal National Institute of

BLIND People (RNIB)
105 Judd Street
London WC1H 9NE
Helpline: 0845 766 9999
Tel: 020 7388 1266
www.rnib.org.uk

Royal National Institute for
Deaf People (RNID)
19-23 Featherstone Street
London EC1Y 8SL
Information Line: 0808 808 0123
Textphone Helpline:0808 808 9000
www.rnid.org.uk

DEVELOPING RELATIONSHIPS

British Association for
Counselling and
Psychotherapy (BACP)
BACP House
15 St John's Business Park
Lutterworth
Leicestershire LE17 4HB
Tel: 01455 883300
www.bacp.co.uk

British Humanist
Association
1 Gower Street
London WC1E 6HD
Tel: 020 7079 3580 www.humanism.org.uk

Carers UK
20 Great Dover Street
London SE1 4LX
Carersline: 0808 808 7777
Tel: 020 7378 4920
www.carersuk.org

Counsel and Care
Twyman House
16 Bonny Street
London NW1 9PG
Advice Line: 0845 300 7585
Tel: 020 7241 8555
www.counselandcare.org.uk

Crossroads Caring for carers
10 Regent Place
Rugby CV21 2PN
Helpline: 01788 573653 www.crossroads.org.uk

Cruse-Bereavement Care
PO Box 800
Richmond
Surrey TW9 1RG
Helpline: 0844 477 9400
Tel: 020 8939 9530
www.crusebereavementcare.org.uk

Family Rights Group
2nd Floor
The Print House
18 Ashwin Street
London E8 3DL

Advice Line: 0800 7311 696
Tel: 020 7923 2628
www.frg.org.uk

Grandparents' Association
Moot House
The Stow
Harlow
Essex CM20 3AG
Helpline: 0845 4349 585
Tel: 0279 428040 www.grandparentsassociation.org.uk

Grandparents Plus
18 Victoria Park Square
London E2 9PF
Tel: 020 8981 8001 www.grandparentsplus.org.uk

Relate
Premier House
Caroline Court
Lakeside Doncaster DN4 5RA
Tel: 0300 100 1234 www.relate.org.uk

United Kingdom Home
Care Association (UKHCA)
2nd Floor Group House
52 Sutton Court Road
Sutton Surrey SM1 4SL
Tel: 020 8288 5291
www.ukhca.co.uk

WRVS (Women's Royal
Voluntary Service)

Garden House
Milton Hill
Abingdon OX13 6AD
Tel: 01235 442900 www.wrvs.org.uk

****

Index

Abbeyfield houses, 32

Activity holidays, 18

Adapting your home, 38, 53

Additional state pension, 110

Advice, Information and Mediation Service for Retirement
Housing, 29

Age Concern, 12, 16, 19, 23, 36, 50, 156, 161

Allowances for blind people, 69

Almshouses, 32

Annuities, 143

Annuity deferral and income withdrawal, 144

Association of British Correspondence Colleges, 14

Association of British Insurers, 22, 152

Attendance Allowance, 42, 59, 62

Bereavement payment, 70

British Association for Sexual and Relationship Therapy, 9

British Trust for Conservation Volunteers, 19

Budgeting Loan, 52

Business structure and tax, 146

Camping, 21

Capital gains Tax, 72

Caravanning, 21

Care and Repair, 49, 53

Care in the home, 55

Cash balance scheme, 118

Chartered Surveyor Voluntary Service, 50

Child Tax Credit, 38, 52

Child Trust Funds, 75

Choosing the right annuity, 143

Christmas bonus, 70

Citizens Advice Bureau, 16, 23, 36, 50
City and Guilds, 13
Civil Partnerships Act 2004, 102
Class 1 contributions, 103
Class 2 contributions, 104
Class 3 contributions, 104
Codicils, 78
Common-law marriage, 76
Community Care Grant, 52
Contracting out, 110
Contributions into occupational schemes, 120
Council tax benefit, 70
Council Tax Benefit, 42
Cyclists Touring Club, 19

Digital Unite, 12
Disability living allowance, 70
Disabled facilities grant, 37, 52
Disabled Living Foundation, 39, 53, 159
Distance learning, 13

Elderly Accommodation Council, 26, 30, 32
Enduring Power of Attorney, 79
Equity release schemes, 40
Estate agents fees, 44
European Health Insurance Card, 22
Executor, 78

Federation of Master Builders, 36
Federation of Master Builders (FMB), 50
Final salary schemes, 116
Foundations, 50

Galleries, 12
Group Pension Scheme, 116
Group personal pension schemes, 123

Health, 22, 48, 154, 161
HM Revenue and Customs, 146
Holidays for carers, 24
Home Improvement Agency, 50
Home Improvement Trust, 52
Home swapping, 21
Housing benefit, 70
Housing Options for Older People, 26
How to claim state pension, 139

Improvements, 35
Income based jobseekers allowance, 52
Income needs in retirement, 83
Income Support, 52
Individual Budgets, 59
Inflation, 84
Inheritance tax, 74, 77
Insurance, 22, 154
Internet, 11, 12, 13, 19, 31, 35, 149

Jobseeker's allowance, 52

Land Registry, 45
Lasting Powers of Attorney, 80
Learn Direct, 13
Learning opportunities, 11
Leasehold Advisory Service, 29
Leaving the country, 140
Libraries, 11, 148

Lifetime lease, 30
Lifetime mortgages, 40
Limits on your pension savings, 114
Long-stay holidays, 20
Lump sum death benefit, 71

Main Inland Revenue limits on pensions., 119
Making a will, 76
Making a Will, 3, 76
Married Couple's allowance, 69
Married couples allowance, 69
MasterBond Warranty, 50
Masters and Johnson, 9
Medical care abroad, 22
Money purchase pension schemes, 117
Money purchase schemes, 117
Museums, 12

National Association For Voluntary and Community action, 16
National Extension College, 13
National Federation of Women's Institutes, 15
National House Building Council, 28
National Insurance, 94, 111
National Savings, 71
National trust, 16
NHS Prescriptions, 48
NHS sight tests, 48

Occupational pensions, 94
Occupational Therapists, 53
Office of the Public Guardian, 80
Open and Distance Learning Quality Council, 14
Open College of Arts, 13

Partnerships, 147

Passport, 48

Payments of personal pensions, 144

Pension credit, 52, 70

Pension Credit, 37, 42

Pension Credit Guarantee, 59

Pension credits, 92

Pensions, 3, 4, 148

Personal allowances, 65

Personal pensions, 97, 135

Planning ahead for care, 63

Planning for the future, 81

Power of attorney, 78

Qualifying for state pension, 102

Qualifying to join an occupational scheme, 116

RADAR, 24, 156

Radio, 12

REACH, 16

Relate, 8, 16, 166

Removal costs, 45

Repairs, 35

Retired and Senior Volunteer Programme, 16

Retirement housing, 26, 27, 60, 158

Retiring early, 141

Retiring from business, 73

Retiring late, 141

Reversion schemes, 41

Right to buy, 31

Running your own business, 146

Salvation Army, 16

Self-employed, 104, 110
Selling your home, 43, 73
SERPS, 91, 110
Sexual relations, 8
Shared ownership housing, 29
Sheltered housing, 55, 60
Social fund, 52
Social services, 52, 53
Special-interest holidays, 18
Specialist tour operators, 19
Stakeholder schemes, 96, 123
Stamp duty land tax, 44
State Earnings Related Pension, 110
Staying Put, 49

Tax, 3, 4, 38, 42, 72, 74, 150, 152
Tax advantages of occupational schemes, 115
Tax in retirement, 135
Tax relief, 65
Tax-free income, 70
Television, 12
Television licence, 49
The Crown, 76
The Law Society, 77
The savings credit, 92
The state pension, 91
Travel, 19, 34, 152, 159
TrustMark, 37, 51

University of the Third Age, 12
Unmarried partners, 76

Victim Support, 16

Voluntary Services Overseas, 21

Will-making kit, 77
Wills, 76
Winter fuel payment, 70
Women's clubs, 15
Worker Educational Associations, 12

****